Theology by Heart

This book is dedicated to my mother,
Elizabeth Sarah Culy Clark

Theology by Heart

Women, the Church and God

Ellen Clark-King

✚ EPWORTH

British Library Cataloguing in Publication data

A catalogue record for this book is available
from the British Library

0 7162 0587 4

First published in 2004
by Epworth Press
4 John Wesley Road
Werrington, Peterborough, PE4 7ZP

Typeset by Rowland Phototypesetting Ltd,
Bury St Edmunds, Suffolk
Printed and bound in Great Britain by
Biddles Ltd, www.biddles.co.uk

CONTENTS

ACKNOWLEDGEMENTS

My thanks are first of all due to the women of St Anthony's estate who so generously shared their feelings and thoughts with me. Their voices are the bedrock of this book and the project would have been impossible without their good-humoured co-operation.

The original research was overseen by Deborah Sawyer and Linda Woodhead of Lancaster University and their encouragement, insight and constructive criticism are central to any success that this research has achieved. Others who have helped refine my thinking include my brother, Jonathan Clark, who commented on chapters with wit and wisdom; Elaine Graham, who also helped in getting the work published; and Natalie Watson, whose enthusiasm for the project has been a constant encouragement. I would also like to thank Mary McClintock Fulkerson for writing the foreword to this book. I am grateful for the financial support of the Diocese of Newcastle in my first year of research and the Arts and Humanities Research Board thereafter.

Finally, my thanks are due to my husband Jeremy, who has supported me with unflagging patience and good humour, providing endless encouragement, wise counsel and occasional chocolate. This book could not have been written without him.

FOREWORD

One of the inescapable logics of liberation theologies of all kinds is that, rather than continuing to reproduce the discourse of the 'experts', theology must attend to 'popular religion'. 'The people' are vital conveyors of the faith. There is more to this logic, however, than simple inclusion. There is wisdom in their faith, especially the faith of the marginalised. Discourses of the common folk not only have integrity; they contain a logic and creativity of their own from which official theology itself should learn if it is to enhance resources for God's justice in the world. If not a surprising observation from the perspective of cultural anthropologists, sociologists and culture theorists, or even common sense, this is truly a challenge to deeply entrenched ways of defining theology – a challenge that feminist theologians have been happy to advance.

Think of the numerous extensions of this logic as liberationist commitments proliferate. Conceptions of what counts as popular religion or the faith of the marginalised continue to expand along with their implications for category-critique. Latin American liberationists and black theologies attended to the poor and to African American communities with accompanying challenges to traditional theology. Feminist theologians argued that women were excluded by theology's marking by male-gendered constructs of the world. Womanists, among others, exposed the imprint of social location on white feminist theology, displaying the function of a race (whiteness) we feminists did not even see that we had, and its power to occlude. More recently queer theology further extends this logic by identifying the heteronormativity in much liberation theology and resulting exclusions.

Theology by Heart by Ellen Clark-King carries forward this ecumenical logic in significant ways, taking up the liberationist challenge in a remarkably accessible style. Writing about 'women who do not fit within the feminist fold nor register on the radar of the vast majority of academic theologians', as she puts it, Clark-King follows out this impulse to complicate accounts of popular religion and, in doing so, demonstrates that the impulse is a profoundly theological one. Her work on British working-class women's piety assumes that God's liberating presence is in the everyday, in the ordinary, and that 'theological reflection' is a practice of all people of faith, not simply those in the academy. Convinced that feminist theology has overlooked working-class women, the author spent considerable time interviewing and interacting with British working-class women from Roman Catholic, Methodist, Anglican and evangelical faith communities. Committed to a dialogue between feminist theology and the very different faith discourse of these women, Clark-King has produced a distinctively respectful account and defence of these working-class women's pieties.

The dialogue is a rich one. It is feminist. Clark-King brings her own passion for feminist theology's discernment to the dialogue and treats major themes of the women's discourses comparatively with feminist theologians' own accounts. With nuanced and careful attention to their faith, she does the constructive work of finding commonalities between feminist themes and the faith of these women. The dialogue is also scrupulously honest. Clark-King is clear about the differences between feminist 'truths' and this working-class faith, and sometimes feminist thinking on issues is truly challenged – especially white-feminism. She finds and honours resources from which women get self-worth in too-easily misinterpreted or overlooked elements of working-class life. The careful way in which Clark-King interprets the continual preference for such feminist 'no-no's' as male God-language, takes seriously the web of meanings that makes up this social location and is invaluable. Not only are the women's social conditions important in her analysis, but the author surfaces potential subtleties in the heterosexual erotic resonances of their God-relations that are frequently missed by feminist analyses. Never falling prey to a romanticisation of these more traditional male-dominated symbols systems, her work is suggestive that there is much more to be gleaned from the gendered and eroticised connotations of this language. In short, feminist theology can be the beneficiary of such pieties.

Finally, Clark-King's dialogue between feminist theology, indeed all academic theology, and these British working-class women of faith is an open-ended one. She challenges us to much more conversation. Neither interlocutor is completely correct, Clark-King insists, neither the feminists nor the women. Nor is it her role – the role of the academic – to provide the synthesis of these sometimes conflicting theologies. Rather *Theology by Heart* illustrates the profound importance of learning from the other. It is a learning which cannot be mere tourism, and it is a learning, indeed a receiving, that does not stop with the closure of conceptualisation. Clark-King has surfaced a new population for the ever-expanding logic of liberation-inflected theologies and recognises that she has been given a gift even as she gives one to readers.

Mary McClintock Fulkerson

INTRODUCTION

I would hate the Church to become middle class. I really would.

I always feel like – picture – that God's got great big long arms, you know, and his arms are always there ready for you. A hug can do wonders, can't it? If you feel down and somebody gives you a hug, it's lovely.

This, this is hell and when you die you go to heaven . . . There must . . . be a better place than this to live in, 'cos there's that many drugs and killings and shootings. Paradise, that's where I think you go to, that's beautiful.

These are voices that belong to working-class women who are regular churchgoers and who live on St Anthony's estate in the East End of the city of Newcastle upon Tyne in North East England. They are voices that are seldom heard in the lecture rooms of academe or the corridors of ecclesiastical power, but they are still voices with something important to say. This book arose from my desire to listen to such new voices – voices that speak of God and prayer and life and the Church with heartfelt intensity, humour and honesty.

I was introduced to these voices, and their distinctive Geordie accent, when I moved to the East End of Newcastle upon Tyne in January 2000. Their particular take on life fascinated me and fired me with a desire to allow their insights and vitality to reach a wider audience. This desire had an academic source as well: I wanted to see whether or not feminist theology could live up to

1

its promise to listen to the voices of people – especially women – who are on the margins of society's power structures. So began a conversation with two very different partners: on one side the working-class women of St Anthony's estate and on the other the middle-class women who write in the field of feminist theology and spirituality. This was a conversation where I found myself listening with fascination to both sides and where, though my background made me a member of the latter group, my new local loyalties made me want to champion the other side.

There were, it must be said, things being voiced by both groups that offered new perspectives on some of the questions currently interesting theological thinkers, and new challenges for the self-understanding of the Church. Should the Church be defined as a space for worship or a workshop for building community and crafting social justice? Should we look for God, and for all possibility of fulfilment, within this world alone or is it still acceptable to hope for a better future in another life? Should our spirituality be defined by our relationships and, if so, which ones? Should we speak of God with male metaphors alone or should these be accompanied, or replaced, by female imagery for the divine? The answers to some of these questions will hopefully become clear in the following pages, though there is still plenty of room left for continuing questioning, and continuing conversations, beyond the end of this book.

It will soon become apparent that my own interests lie primarily in the area of feminist and liberation theology. It is these schools of theology that are most open to the challenge of listening to previously excluded voices; both, indeed, are built on the premise that theology has excluded too many such voices in the past. The focus in feminist theology, quite obviously, is on allowing women's voices to be heard, while liberation theologians have traditionally turned their attention to the poor and marginalised, particularly in Latin America and the Third World. Each has been criticised for allowing its focus to be too constrained – for example, in the past, feminist theology was accused of ignoring issues of race and class, while male liberation theologians stood accused of ignoring issues of gender. In both schools it was all too easy to allow new orthodoxy to take the place of the old and become overly protective of past insights.

However, both schools also have built into them the possibility of movement and growth because both take as their starting point the centrality of experience to doing theology. This means that they are theoretically open to taking account of experiences of God from within the Church that they had previously not been aware of or not considered worthy of focused attention. When a new, or previously overlooked, lived experience of God is brought to their attention, then they have the tools to build it into their theology, as well as having the tools to challenge experiences of God that appear inauthentic or untrue to the revelation of God in the person of Jesus Christ and in the continued teaching of the Holy Spirit. I would want to characterise the theology that I do as arising from both these schools and being a 'theology of spirituality' – in other words, a theology that is based on the lived experience of God within the Church. Just as this lived experience differs greatly from one area, and one person, to the next, this theology is one that is comfortable with a multitude of voices contributing to the song of God's glory in their own distinctive way.

Basing theology on the lived experience of God has another important benefit: by including the experience of the whole person, rather than just their intellect, it allows for a theology that is as much of the heart as of the mind. Theology is not compartmentalised, kept separate from the rest of the spiritual life, but becomes part of our everyday reflection on our relationship with God. In this way, it becomes the task of the whole people of God rather than only those with higher degrees. It also becomes the task of the whole person rather than the intellect alone. This sort of theology is not locked away in esoteric textbooks but is to be found in every church that takes its Christian living seriously.

So, this is a book of feminist theology not because it chooses from the beginning to echo the orthodoxy of feminist theological thought, but because it chooses to be true to the underlying motivation of feminist writing. This is the need to listen to the people who are on the outside rather than the inside – in this particular case, those on the outside of the Church, the theological academy and feminism itself due to their class, age and education. This book invites the whole Church to listen attentively to these voices and learn from their spiritual experiences. It has been written with the intention that it be accessible to readers unfamiliar with theological or feminist jargon. Its most vivid passages, however, are those where my own words don't figure at all – they are the passages where the women's voices tell their own stories and their own truths in indomitable Geordie style. It is the passion and depth of faith these quotes contain that demand our respect and attention. It is these voices that illuminate our understanding of God and provoke us to think again about our own Christian journeys.

LISTENING TO OTHERS

Feminist theologians, in my opinion, cannot continue to base theologies on conjectures, presumptions and hunches, not even when they concern the experiences of our own immediate group. We will have to *ask* people what they feel, religiously as in other areas of life.[1]

Lene Sjørup is here making a point that is central not only to feminist theology but also all theology that takes the lived experience of God as its starting point. It is not enough to guess at, let alone rely on our assumptions about, the religious experiences of even those people who are closest to us. Theologians, both in the Church and in the academy, need to hear the voices of those who live out their faith day by day and especially the voices of those who do so far from the centres of theological power. This chapter explores the ways in which such voices can be heard most faithfully and the attempts that need to be made to lessen the inevitable distortion that occurs when we try to speak for others.

It was very apparent that, before listening to the voices of others, I needed to be aware of my own motivation in undertaking the research and the possible influence this and other factors of my personal experience might have on how I interpreted what I was hearing. It is a commonplace of social science research, especially in its feminist forms, that the researcher can never be a mere mirror reflecting an entirely accurate picture of her subject's lives. The researcher is always a filter for the material, which will be in some ways changed in its passage from the interviewee to the written page. This distortion can be kept to a minimum by reflective self-awareness on behalf of the researcher – listening in an interview situation to one's own reactions to the speaker as well as to what is being said. In order for you to be aware of ways in which my own experiences may be colouring the material, it is useful for you to know something about me. In this way both writer and reader are reminded that the writing is necessarily subjective and have the necessary insight to identify the locations where subjectivity is most apparent.

Before studying for a doctorate, I had spent four and a half years as Chaplain and Fellow of a Cambridge college enjoying the stimulating company of students, staff and fellows alike, but feeling increasingly isolated from what counts for most as 'normal' life. I had just completed an MA in Christian Spirituality at Heythrop College, London, and wanted to combine my continuing interest in spirituality with a return to a less academic, and less elite, environment. My husband, another Anglican priest, also felt very strongly that he wanted to work in a parish that had different needs from the middle-class or rural locations of his ministry so far. This is what brought us to live in St Anthony's among the community and churches described in the next chapter.

One module of the MA course that I found particularly interesting was that based on the diverse material being produced by the feminist spirituality industry, the bulk of which came from the United States. I was at one and the same time excited to hear the voices of women speaking about their spirituality and yet disappointed that it seemed to be such a narrow selection of women – white, middle-class and part of the academy – who were actually being heard. There were, though, a few exceptions to this rule. In the work of Mujerista theologians from Latin America and Minjung theologians from Asia, along with black womanist writers from the United States, it was possible to hear exceptions to the white affluent majority. There were even a few fascinating studies that listened to white women who were outside the feminist middle-class loop.[2] However, these were all based in the United States and it seemed that there was nothing being written on the spiritual experiences of British working-class women. These were the people among whom I was now living and whose outspoken opinions on a vast array of subjects were a pleasure, or occasional penance, to listen to on every bus journey or visit to the local shops.

The impact of class was impossible to miss from the moment I moved into St Anthony's. It was my first time living, for anything more than a few months, in an area with a monochrome white working-class, or under-class, population. It was my first experience of being an outsider in my immediate social context. I was aware as I walked down the street that I dressed differently from the women around me, that my body shape was different (for the first time I, at 5 foot 3 inches, felt tall) and that I did not understand the social code by which local relationships were organised. More than anything, it was my voice that set me apart – as a Southerner, as a member of a different class, as a woman who occasionally employed cleaners rather than working as one. My growing consciousness of my own social and educational privilege and the limitations of my own class viewpoint made me increasingly determined to try to listen to voices so different from my own and see what they had to teach me.

In order to listen to these women, I organised a study founded on semi-structured interviews and participant observation. I was already a member of the congregation of St Aidan's (the names of all the churches and individuals in this book have been changed in order to protect the participants' anonymity as far as possible) – the Anglican church where my husband was vicar, a situation that lasted a few months before the diocese found me a parish in which to minister that was a few miles away. I was made very welcome at St Aidan's in my role as the vicar's wife, though the church was not prepared to accept my ministry as a woman priest. I also spent time in Green Memorial Methodist Church, St Mark's (Anglican) and the Roman Catholic Church of St Justin's, taking part in services as a member of the congregation when free from my duties as non-stipendiary priest at a parish in North Shields.

As well as the church involvement, I became Treasurer for the East End Women's Forum – a group of local women and community workers organising the annual Women's Day celebrations for Byker and Walker – and this brought me into contact with women who had no church affiliation. In each of these environments there was a ready welcome and willingness to accept any contribution that I could make to their endeavours.

There was no difficulty in finding women who were prepared to talk to me about their spiritual lives – at least in three of the four churches – but the process of selecting interviewees varied from one congregation to the next. In St Aidan's, where I knew the women already, it was easy for me to ask them personally if they would be interested in taking part. Their response was usually positive, mainly from a wish to help me out, though one woman was quite clear that she did not want to be involved. At St Mark's, the small congregation was easy to get to know and, because of their evangelical tradition, were happy to share their faith with a newcomer. At the end of one of the services, I asked for anyone who was interested to tell me, and about half the women in the congregation volunteered. In St Justin's, the process was different. I had first asked permission of Father Steven to carry on my research in the church, which had been readily granted. Sister Theresa then went round the congregation before mass one Sunday, with me tagging along behind, and asked a range of women if they would be prepared to take part. It was hard for them to say no to such an enthusiastic nun, but, in any case, there was a general willingness to be interviewed.

The only church in which I encountered problems finding inter-viewees was Green Memorial Methodist. The minister there was very happy for me to use the church for the research and was also keen for me to take services occasionally. In fact, I avoided doing so on all but one occasion as I did not want to influence the women with my own spirituality.[3] I tried asking for volunteers in one of the services, as I had at St Mark's, but this time there was only one response. I then attended a number of meetings of the weekly Family Meeting Point until I felt that the women were used to my being around. I then asked individuals at the meeting if they would take part, but again there was only refusal. The women showed a greater degree of diffidence about expressing their own views on faith and prayer than the other congregations and did not seem to feel that they had anything to contribute. The only exception to this, apart from the volunteer already mentioned, was the community worker at the church, who was happy to take part. This means that the Methodist viewpoint is under-represented compared to those of the other churches. I attempted to counter-balance the shortage of individual interviews by attending the Family Meeting Point on a regular basis for some months in order to gain as great an insight as possible into the spirituality and faith life of the Methodist women. This proved reasonably successful, but I still regret not having more personal Methodist stories to tell.

The interviews themselves followed a semi-structured pattern. This allowed me to ensure that I covered the areas I needed to, while allowing flexibility to enable the interviews to become conversations rather than interrogations. Each interview was very different, with the order in which issues were discussed changing with the flow of each encounter. There were, of course, some women who talked easily with little prompting from me, others who needed more frequent prompts and some whose flow of conversation threatened to overwhelm the interview and, indeed, the interviewer. Each interview was recorded, with the interviewee's permission, using an unobtrusive dictaphone. The interviews were then transcribed by myself – a process that got slightly quicker with time but was still arduous and time-consuming. It did, however, help to guarantee the anonymity of the participants and also provided me with a greater familiarity with the material than would otherwise have been the case. In the transcriptions, I attempted to capture the flow of the conversation as accurately as possible, including the pauses, indeterminate noises and repetitions that give a flavour of the ease or difficulty with which different questions were answered.

The interviews usually took place in the women's own homes. There were two exceptions to this rule with women who felt more comfortable meeting me in the vicarage. I preferred to go to them, partly because the home environment gave me a greater insight into their lives and partly because being on their territory seemed to offset slightly the power relationship between interviewer and interviewee. They were more in control of the situation, could choose to break the interview for tea or talk to someone else in the house and gained authority from their role as host. There were occasional interruptions, but, in general, the women had carefully set aside time when they would not be disturbed or overheard. It was a great pleasure to me when many of the women said at the end of the interviews that they had enjoyed the whole process and found that they had much more to say about their faith than they expected. I had been anxious that they might find my interest in them exploitative, but this did not seem to be the case. Instead, there was a sense that it was a mutually beneficial conversation that gave them the rare opportunity to be listened to with respect and close attention and to talk about matters that were close to their hearts.

During the interviews themselves, I was very conscious of my own position as a middle-class woman and member of the clergy. The interviewees all knew that I was an Anglican priest and I was always aware of the possibility that this might have inhibited them in their answers to some of my questions. However, this did not seem to happen. When asked to tell me their beliefs about the role of women in the Church, those who did not accept women priests often presaged their comments with an apology, but did not change their views to suit the listener. The most apologetic way of phrasing this was probably that of Vera, a member of St Justin's:

Well, a lot of people seem to think that it would be nice to have women priests but I'm, I'm from the old school and I – with all due respect, Ellen, honestly – I just think that, you know, a man, usually, is the priest. I'm talking about our faith, our church, Ellen, with all due respect to you, honestly please.

While aware of the possibility of giving offence, the women interviewed were also aware that honesty was being asked of them and
did not seem inhibited about speaking their minds.

My response to the women I was meeting was one of great
respect, which grew the better I got to know them. I was often
moved by the stories they had to tell – both those about the
circumstances of their own lives and those about their relationship
with God and the divine. These were individuals with depths of
lived experience and spiritual encounter that were rarely revealed.
The majority of them met life with courage and humour, refusing
to be patronised by a society that judged them to have fallen short
of its ideals of success and accomplishment. This is not to say that
they were all happy with how life had treated them – there were
often tears during the interviews as well as laughter. They were
not private people as a whole, often willing to share the intimate
details of their latest illness and hospital treatment with a relish
for the gory far beyond my own. I am ashamed to think how
cheaply such women are often spoken of by my colleagues in
college common rooms and in some clergy gatherings and to know
that I have shared in such belittling. At least my research has
reminded me of one thing – that insight and wisdom are not
confined to academia and the Church has a great resource in its
pews if only it can learn to utilise it.

There are those who would seriously question the possibility of
any valid research resulting from a study where there is a gulf –
whether of race, colour, class, culture or gender – between the researcher and the researched. In the words of American womanist
writer bell hooks:

Often this speech about the 'Other' annihilates, erases: 'no need
to hear your voice when I can talk about you better than you
can speak about yourself. No need to hear your voice. Only tell
me about your pain. I want to know your story. And then I
will tell it back to you in a new way. Tell it back to you in such
a way that it has become mine, my own ... I am still the

coloniser, the speaking subject, and you are now at the centre of my talk.'[4]

However, as the feminist ethnographic researchers Sue Wilkinson and Celia Kitzinger point out,[5] if this injunction is taken seriously, then feminist ethnography is in danger of only speaking about white, middle-class experience and omitting other voices altogether – until the utopian time when every social group is enabled to speak for itself. It also contains the danger that defining the 'us' for whom we are qualified to speak will result in the extreme reductionism described by Linda Alcoff as '"Communities" composed of single individuals'.[6]

The other essays in Wilkinson and Kitzinger's collection deal in a variety of ways with the tensions that speaking for the other brings to research. Marian Titley and Becky Chasey in their article 'Across differences of age: young women speaking of and with old women'[7] confront the tension head on:

> To avoid openly discussing old women protects us from the charge of 'wrongful representation', while seeming to credit us with acknowledging the limits of our professional and personal experience. However, by avoiding this risk we are complicit in the continued devaluing of old women's experiences. Both we and they are then silenced.[8]

Not speaking for the other can be the safe option, preserving the researcher from all charges of misrepresentation and colonial consumption of the other's experience and insights. However, for myself, as for Titley and Chasey, this option feels like opting out, which only serves to extend the silence.

There is no obvious or easy solution to the problem of speaking for the other, but, if we want to hear the voices of those who cannot yet gain a hearing in their own right, it is still necessary to make the attempt. There are ethical practices that can help us to limit the risks of a colonising takeover of the researched by the researcher. Primary among these is the reflexive self-awareness of the researcher herself and her willingness to allow her presence to be seen in the research. There is no ethnography in which the filter of the researcher is not present; the necessity is to show that filter for what it is rather than deny its existence.

I have, therefore, allowed my voice and my experience to be a presence in the writing of this book and attempted to be aware of their influence during the practice of the research itself. When visiting the churches and church groups, I was conscious of my own personal preferences and tried to make allowances for these. It has meant that I have maintained a careful awareness of my own reactions to the women and their responses to my questions during the interviews. A continual monitoring of their vocabulary, and of my own, helped to ensure that we were understanding one another. If I was unsure of their meaning, I would reflect back what I thought I had heard to see if they agreed or if I needed to modify my understanding. In all this I could only be honest about who I am: it would have been counterproductive in every way for me to pretend that I had more in common with the women than was the case. So I kept my Southern dialect and did not attempt to talk of children as 'bairns' or replace my instinctive 'yes' with the local 'aye'. It seemed that, in being honest myself – responding truthfully to questions put to me by the interviewees, for example – I would be best able to establish an honest response on both sides.

The hope was that such honesty would provide the best foundation for the open sharing of the women's real experiences of God, the Church, prayer and so on. 'Women's experience' has been at the heart of the feminist theological endeavour from the beginning – indeed, it can be claimed that the 'second wave' of feminist theory in the 1960s began with the discovery of 'women's experience' as a distinct category.[9] This happened as a result of the publication of books such as Simone de Beauvoir's *The Second Sex* and Betty Friedan's *The Feminine Mystique* and the consciousness-raising movement, in which groups of women found that they recognised their own stories in each other's lives. The experiences that these women began to perceive as common between them were marginalisation and oppression, of being shunted to the sidelines in the game of life while men took for themselves the roles of the main players. Women began to see themselves as another group whose interests had been overlooked by patriarchy[10] and who needed to mobilise politically in order to assert their claim to equality.

As the influence of feminism spread into the theological academy, so 'women's experience' became an important category in theology. This happened as part of a larger movement within theology that was rediscovering the significance of experiences previously ignored within theological thought. The overarching title for such types of theology is 'liberation theology' and within this category can be found emphases on the experiences of the poor, the socially and politically marginalised, black people, colonised people, gays and lesbians, as well as on the experiences of women per se. The motivation behind such theology did not lie purely, or even primarily, in the search for eternal truths about God, but, rather, in the need for a way of thinking about God that promoted social action in the here and now. Its rallying cry has been 'orthopraxis' – right action – rather than 'orthodoxy' – right believing.

Liberation and feminist theologians did not believe that they were doing anything new by working from experience; what they did believe was revolutionary was the focus on experiences from outside the centres of ecclesiastical and academic power – the poor instead of the wealthy, black instead of white, women instead of men. In the words of Rosemary Radford Ruether, 'What has been called the objective source of theology, Scripture and tradition, are themselves codified collective human experience.'[11] Feminists and liberationists were not providing a radically new basis for theology but making its foundation visible and expanding it to include areas that had previously been ignored.

It could not be said that all theologians would agree with the emphasis placed on experience within liberation theology. Many would prefer to stress the role of revelation, especially questioning a definition of the Bible that emphasised human experience over divine activity. However, many theologians within liberation theology, myself included, would see such a dichotomy as false. Divine revelation is not denied. However, it is understood as being both apprehended and filtered through human experience. To put it another way, in speaking for God, the ultimate other, there is bound to be the same interference from our own preconceptions and limited vision that infects any speaking for the other. This is not the same as saying that there is no communication from God to humanity, but only that such communication takes place within the limitations of humanity's ability to communicate. God's Word always speaks through human mouths.

It is a theological truism that the study of God cannot fully progress if it is separated from the study of human beings, as well as that humanity cannot be truly understood without an understanding of God. It follows from this that our understanding of God will be severely limited if we only take the experiences of certain human beings seriously. The American feminist theologian Mary McClintock Fulkerson makes this same point using the starting point of the *imago Dei* (the doctrine that human beings are all made in the image of God). She insists that all human lives have the potential to reveal something of the grace and nature of God and our image of God will remain incomplete unless we attend to all such revelations: 'The continued approbation of reality as God's requires from us the capacity to see grace in the lives of those who speak of God's way under the adverse conditions we rarely or never live in.'[12]

Fulkerson is primarily addressing the feminist theological community – encouraging them to listen to women outside feminism, those who are even antagonistic towards it. She speaks of hearing the voices of the women 'who are not the "we" of the feminist account'[13] and attending to the 'emancipatory possibilities' that they have discovered in their own circumstances. This same attention and listening should come from the community of the wider Church. Theology is not an activity that should be limited to academic professionals – learning to understand God better is the job of the whole Church. In order to achieve this, the Church needs to take seriously the experiences of all its members, regardless of their level of education, social class, race, age or gender.

It must be admitted that even within feminist theology – where women's experiences were supposed to be at the heart of the endeavour – it has always been easier to hear some voices over those of others. An example of those who felt ignored by mainstream feminist theologians – at least in the early days of feminist theology – is black American women.[14] The writer Alice Walker coined the term 'womanist' to distinguish the writings of black feminists from those of their white counterparts, whom, it was felt, had not thrown off their racism along with their gender oppression. Their main criticism was that white feminists were universalising white, and middle-class, women's experiences without taking into account the effects of race and class on those experiences. These criticisms were aimed at feminist theology as well as the other branches of feminist theory. In the words of the womanist theologian Jacquelyn Grant, 'Feminist theology is inadequate for two reasons: it is *White* and *racist*.'[15]

Grant is led to this conclusion by her belief that white feminist theology ignores the gulf that slavery and segregation have put between the experiences of white and black American women. It is an argument echoed by bell hooks in the secular sphere in her classic book of 1981 *'Ain't I a Woman?' Black Women and Feminism*.[16] An example of the kind of universalising hooks and others object to can be seen in the assumptions that white feminists make about the inherent link between the natural world and women. Mary Daly, among many others, sees a natural connection between women and all that is natural and outside the control of man-made culture and technology. Identification with the natural is seen as liberating for white women, allowing them to connect with their bodies and move away from the artifices of femininity. However,

16

nature occupies a different place in many black women's experience. It has often been hostile – the enemy from which a living
has to be dragged – and has also formed a part of the dehumanising
caricatures of black women as beasts of burden, subject to animal
lusts and the antithesis of the pure, cultured white lady. It is not
surprising, then, that black women do not usually take the natural
world as the springboard of their theological reconstruction: 'white
women have found in nature a sister and a source of reunification
of the separations they experience as women; while black women
have taken the conflicts of urban civilisation as their point of
departure'.[17]

The criticism from black women was heard within the feminist
community as the introduction to *Weaving the Visions* – Christ
and Plaskow's anthology of women's spirituality, which followed
ten years after *Womanspirit Rising*: 'Ten years later we recognise that
the term "women's experience" too often means "white middle-
class women's experience", in just the same way that "human"
too often means "male"'.[18] It seems to me that it is time for the
Church to make the same confession of a limited ability to hear
experiences outside the middle-class, and male, mainstream and,
furthermore, to make a new effort to listen actively to the voices
it has disregarded in the past.

One of the most important recent challenges to the use of
experience within theology – or any other branch of the humanities
and social sciences – has come from postmodernism. It is not my
intention here to go into the complicated debate concerned at any
length, but just to point to how it impinges on this work. This it
does most directly in its killing of, in the words of Seyla Benhabib,
'the autonomous, self-reflective subject'.[19] The death of such a subject means that experience can no longer be considered the simple
possession of an individual that they can communicate directly to
any other rational human being. Experience is no longer understood as something the subject has direct and unencumbered access
to, but as something that is always already qualified by the subject's
view of him or herself and the world.

There is another way in which postmodernism has impinged on experience, and this is by its habitual stance of relativising and fragmenting all knowledge. It, therefore, becomes difficult to talk about any shared experience as the differences rather than the commonalities between people and what they feel are emphasised. The feminist thinker Nancy Fraser points to a possible way forward that, while allowing postmodern ideas to influence feminism, does not allow them to paralyse it. Central to her argument is the premise that feminism is a political movement rather than a purely intellectual exercise. In other words, its intention is to do and change rather than just analyse and comment. This prompts her to favour a pragmatic approach to feminist theory, one that is flexible enough to be adaptable to different needs in different circumstances. In particular, this means keeping the tools of post-modernism that allow us to question old certainties, while not losing sight of the end to which this questioning is hoping to lead – a society that allows the flourishing of both women and men: 'Feminists need both deconstruction *and* reconstruction, destabilis-ation of meaning *and* projection of utopian hope.'[20] What Fraser says of feminists is equally true for other forms of experience-based theology that are as interested in action as reflection.

We need to keep the category 'experience', but we also need to understand that this is not a simple concept. Joan Scott – looking at the use of experience within the context of writing about history – provides us with a very usable theory of experience. She sees it as part of the process of constructing a subject rather than as a possession of the subject to which they have direct access: 'It is not individuals who have experience, but subjects who are constituted through experience.'[21] Experience becomes that which needs expla-nation rather than the unproblematic foundation of our expla-nation. We need to be aware of the impact of ideology on the formation of the person who recounts their experiences and be aware of the part this may have played in the way that they present and interpret their experiences, to themselves as well as to the other.

If, as Scott persuasively argues, we are indeed 'subjects constituted through experience', then our religious subjectivity should also be seen as being constituted through experience. Our understanding of spirituality, and of God, grows out of the nexus of our life experience, which cannot escape being influenced by our gender, class and worshipping community, as well as the individual minutiae of our own life path. This is an immanent formation of spirituality, although traditional Christian thinking, in agreement with the women in the interviews, would assert that it was immanent experience of a still transcendent reality. This accords with Lene Sjørup's statement that 'the basis of theology is personal experiences of the holy'[22] and this is as available to the women of St Anthony's estate as it is to theologians in the academy. Scott does not move us back to a time when experience could be naïvely assumed to be immediately available to the individual and readily communicated to another. Instead, she moves us forward to a point where experience is problematic but, notwithstanding this, still central to our understanding of the production of selves and, therefore, the production of knowledge.

This use of experience also fits in well with the ethics of the research that were discussed earlier. It means that I, as the researcher, need to be constantly aware of the place that my ideology and the experiences that have contributed to my construction of self impact on my interpretation of the life stories that are recounted to me. It also means that I need to be aware that the experiences recounted are not simple facts but events that are already themselves interpreted by the speaker. One further point that Beverley Skeggs emphasises in her work *Formations of Class and Gender*, which will shortly be looked at in more detail, is that it is not just the large-scale experiences that are important, but also all the mundane details of life that contribute to the construction of the self: 'Whereas an event can produce explanations of identity, the mundane reiterative everyday experiences of living degradation and negative value positioning often cannot ... However, this study has shown that it is precisely the everyday negotiations of the mundane that do matter, that are formative, that do count.'[23]

Joan Scott's thinking differs from that of some other post-structuralist theorists by claiming a continuing place for the subject and so for political endeavour: 'This kind of approach does not undercut politics by denying the existence of subjects, it instead interrogates the processes of their creation . . . and opens new ways for thinking about change.'[24] Scott has placed experience at the heart of the creation of subjects and the production of knowledge in order to rethink feminist historiography; I have placed it there in order to think theologically in new and authentic ways.

The focus of this book, as will become increasingly clear in the course of the following chapters, is the experience of a group of women considered to be marginal in the wider life and power structures of the Church, but faithful members of that Church for many years. Taking Scott's insights and allying them with the insights of liberation theology, I believe that the women's accounts can give us access to the way that they inhabit the image of God and so show us an often disregarded facet of God's image in our world. This is not because they 'possess' the experiences and can hand them on unchanged, but because they *are* their experiences and, in sharing them, partial and packaged as their accounts may be, they share something of their personhood. In listening to their voices, recorded as closely as possible to the original, we are able to hear something unique.

'It doesn't matter what party's in power, it's always the working class that's hit hardest.'[25] Class seldom gets a mention in theological writings. There is, of course, a great deal written about the 'bias for the poor' of liberation theology – both by those in favour and those against. However, class as a category for thinking about people is decidedly unfashionable. It seems that many people in the UK today assume that class distinctions no longer have any real existence or validity. We are all 'middle class', whether upper, middle or lower-middle, apart from those on the margins who have opted out of, or been dropped from (delete as your political preferences suggest) modern society altogether.

It is not surprising, therefore, that questions of class and Church are seldom brought together. The one major exception to this is the work of those looking at urban theology and the role of the Church in areas of urban deprivation, but, even here, it is deprivation that is the focus of the work, rather than class per se. However, as the quote at the beginning of the last paragraph illustrates, class is part of the self-understanding of the people of St Anthony's. Interestingly, some of the women expressed in their interviews a fear that their sense of themselves as working-class would put a growing barrier between them and the Church. In the words of Susan, a member of St Justin's: 'I would hate the Church to become middle class. I really would.' So class plays a central role in the way that the women see themselves and their world.

One of the clearest writers on the effects of class in the UK is Beverley Skeggs, a social scientist focusing on ethnography and women's studies. Her major work, *Formations of Class and Gender*,[26] is the result of a 12-year study of 83 young, working-class women identified by their participation in Caring courses at the local college of further education. It is a deeply felt book that has been, in her own words, 'fuelled by passion and anger'.[27] Her aims are, in some ways, very close to my own: 'to enable the experiences of working-class women and men, Black and White, to be seen as legitimate and valued and hence taken seriously'.[28]

Skeggs is able to build from her study of the women's experience – which, like Scott, she sees as constituting them as subjects – a convincing account of the way in which they negotiate the small amounts of social, economic, cultural and symbolic capital that accrue to their class and gender position.[29] They are shown as being motivated by a desire to fit into a definition of respectability that allows them to distance themselves from society's view of working-class women as sexually loose and threatening. This involves the creation of a self that is caring and feminine, hetero-sexually orientated and sees membership of the working class as identical with social and economic failure. Throughout the book, there is an emphasis on the lack of alternative positions for these women to adopt, along with a continued alienation from the position that they were actually in.

Being working class does not appear to be so problematic for the women I interviewed. They have a strong sense of identity with the local area and value the community of which they are part, even when they deplore some of the changes that they have seen. There is certainly no hesitation in speaking of the estate as working-class – 'working-class areas like ours', as Rose described it – or describing their families in this way – 'Yes, I came from a working-class family', as Ruth said. Class is a reality for them, as for the women in Skegg's study, but being working-class is definitely not seen in purely negative terms.

It is possible to find a small amount of theology in which class is taken into account as a factor. One of the most impressive writers in this group is Mary McClintock Fulkerson. Her major work, *Changing the Subject: Women's Discourses and Feminist Theology,*[30] is based on her commitment to keeping, but at the same time radically redefining, the subject 'woman' so that it takes account of such differences as class and race. Fulkerson, unlike many feminist writers in theology and other disciplines, is prepared to listen to the voices of women who do not identify with feminist goals. She is very aware of the limitations of viewpoints that adhere to all social positions and, as has already been said, is committed to including all types of human being within the *imago Dei.*

This idea that all human viewpoints are limited is a central plank of experientially based theology in general. It forces theologians to take their own social positionings as seriously as those of the people they are writing about or for. It re-emphasises the point that there is no 'view from nowhere', no disinterested position that any commentator can occupy, from which we can claim to have a 'God's-eye view' of reality. This means that we have to take seriously the notion that our gender, race and class will have limited the ways in which we experience, know and live our faith. Also that, in order to understand our faith most fully, we will need to listen to a multitude of different voices.

One of the major contributions that liberation theologies, including feminist theology, have made to the academy is this insistence on the need to listen to voices from outside the ivory towers. This is of particular importance in the study of theology, which cannot flourish in isolation from the believing community, the vast majority of whom are situated far outside university lecture rooms. Theology, unlike Religious Studies, is a discipline that demands engagement with belief – it is located within, rather than outside, its own field of study. At least, it ought to be.

Unfortunately, it often seems to be the case that the Church – defined as the people who make up the Body of Christ rather than the institution or its leaders – and the theological academy are speaking entirely different languages. This does not immediately matter so much for theology that bases its words about God on unchanging sources of revelation – the Bible or the past writings of the great teachers of the Christian tradition (often referred to as the 'Doctors of the Church'). It is possible for theologians with these foundations to argue that the Church in the present age has simply failed to understand the unchanging truths of God. While this may be lamentable – both because it suggests a degree of arrogance and it divides the 'enlightened' from the rest – it doesn't undermine the rationale on which they are working. Their theological sources are separate from the contemporary life of the Church and, while ignoring the life of the Church may seem short-sighted and limiting, it does not prevent the continued study of their base material.

However, the situation is somewhat different with all theology that looks to experience as an essential part of its source material. If it is cut off from the Church, then it is cut off from the very foundation of its theologising. The damaging effects of such a divide can be seen in South American liberation theology and feminist theology, especially white American and European feminist theology. In the former, as will be discussed in more detail in Chapter 6, there has been a recognition just recently that the liberation theology movement had been more interested in preaching to than listening to the marginalised Christians it was attempting to serve. This has contributed to its, at least partial, failure to become the popular movement for change and empowerment that it hoped to be. In a similar way, there have been signs within feminist theology of a move towards theory that has left it mired in jargon so impenetrable as to cut it off entirely from all but other academics. This is obviously a wrong turn for a theology that takes as its basic premise the value of all women and is fundamentally concerned with listening to those outside conventional power structures. At least, if we accept that theory does need serious discussion, it should keep its place as a means rather than an end of feminist, and other liberation, theology.

It seems to me that it is a fundamental mistake to see theology as the possession of the academy. One of the gifts of feminist theology has been its accentuation of the importance of theology as an embodied and passionate process, rather than one that is purely cerebral and logical. This is not to say that the mind and logical thinking should be devalued or ignored, but that the incarnate God is engaged with the whole person of emotion and body as well as of rationality. Theology, therefore, should also be the product of the whole person in engagement with God rather than just the head alone.

The corollary of this is that theology should not be seen as the possession solely of those who have proved themselves as excelling in thought. It is doubtless true that the great minds of every generation have something to teach the rest of us about the reality of God and our relationship with God. The Church will continue to need 'Doctors' who can think through the implications of its beliefs, but it will also continue to need those who excel in areas other than abstract thinking and theorising. Those who feel the presence of God within their lives, whose spiritual insights are honed by years of quietly faithful Christian living, who commit themselves to work for the coming of the Kingdom by undertaking acts of risky love: these people, as well as the great thinkers, have something to teach the Church about the nature of God and our relationship with God.

This is the joy and potential of a theology that takes experience seriously. It calls out for the gap between Church and academy to be bridged so that the whole people of God can do theology together rather than ignore each other's questions and insights. It will become clear in the succeeding chapters that there is much to be gained from an approach that is willing to listen rather than wanting to dictate. In the pews, there is a wealth of theological experience, some of which has been reflected on over many years, that can only serve to enrich our theological thought. There is far greater hope for a thinking and dynamic Church if there is an integration of academy and pews than if their current mutual disengagement continues.

The experience of doing the research for this book – of living in this area and meeting these people – has been one of immense richness for myself. I have been privileged to hear the spiritual stories of women who have engaged with their faith over many years and in circumstances that have been hard and demanding. I have been welcomed into a community and allowed access to deep experiences of both joy and sadness, as well as the mundane littleness that makes up so much of everyday life.

Two of the most important foundations for the doing of this research have been honesty and self-awareness or reflexivity. The former is the only possible foundation for a relationship that respects the researched as much as the researcher. The women in this study all knew who I was and what I was doing, and any questions that they asked during the interviews or at other times were given honest answers. It is possible that they may have found their own honesty inhibited by my being a priest, but this did not appear to be the case. During the interviews I constantly tried to be aware of the impact that my own experiences and prejudices were having on my understanding and interpretation of the material. This cannot remove all traces of subjectivity from the research, but it can serve to make such subjectivity apparent and render the researcher as well as the researched visible to the reader. Both the researcher and the researched are limited, as well as enabled, by their particular standpoint and neither can rightly claim to have a 'God's-eye view' of reality. Accepting situatedness does not mean abandoning all claims to truth, but is merely an acknowledgement of the partiality of any one viewpoint and the consequent need to build up a vision of truth that incorporates other's angles and insights.

This is the essential basis of theology that takes the human experience of God as one of its most fundamental starting points. Using Joan Scott's theorising as a base, experience is not seen as an unproblematic possession of the individual to which they have direct access and from which they can communicate directly to another. Instead, it is seen as being part of what constitutes the person, as productive of subjects as well as productive of knowledge. In this book, the experiences of this group of white, working-class, Geordie women is mined for the insight they can give into the way that they inhabit the *imago Dei* and the liberative and oppressive operations of faith and spirituality within their lives. Indeed, this insistence on the image of God being present, however clouded, in every human life provides the theological underpinning for this whole endeavour.

The project of hearing others into speech is not a straightforward one. It runs the risk of colonising the other's experiences and distorting their voices to fit in with the harmony, or discord, that the researcher hopes to hear. However, to shy away from such work on the grounds that it might prove troubling is no solution either, as to do so merely leaves others in silence until society as a whole grants them a voice of their own. White, working-class women are 'others' as far as academic theology – feminist or otherwise – is concerned. They are also 'others' in the power structures of the Church, despite their numerical importance. The hope of this book is that, as a result of the experience of listening to these outsiders, both Church and academy will learn what a rich theological resource they have sitting quietly in the wings or, in this case, the pews. This joint listening may also have the highly desirable effect of bringing Church and academy closer together in a joint realisation of how much they have to give to and receive from one another.

Notes

1 Lene Sjørup, *Oneness: A Theology of Women's Religious Experiences*, Leuven: Peeters, 1998, p. 10. Emphasis as in the original.

2 For example, Brenda Brasher, *Godly Women: Fundamentalism and Female Power*, New Brunswick: Rutgers University Press, 1998; Mary McClintock Fulkerson, *Changing the Subject: Women's Discourses and Feminist Theology*, Minneapolis: Fortress, 1994. R. Marie Griffith, *God's Daughters: Evangelical Women and the Power of Submission*, Berkeley: University of California Press, 1997.

3 I did take services elsewhere on the Methodist circuit, which helped keep the relationship positive.

4 Quoted by Wilkinson and Kitzinger (eds), *Representing the Other*, p. 11; from bell hooks, *Yearning: Race, Gender and Cultural Politics*, Boston: South End, 1990, pp. 151–2.

5 In their article 'Theorising representing the other', which introduces the collection of short essays they edited, *Representing the Other*, London, Sage, 1996.

6 Quoted in *Representing the Other*, p. 12.

7 *Representing the Other*, pp. 147–151.

8 *Representing the Other*, p. 148.

9 For a good overview of the development of second wave feminism, see Imelda Whelehan, *Modern Feminist Thought*, New York: New York University Press, 1995.

10 Defined by Elizabeth Schüssler Fiorenza as 'not just ideological dualism or androcentric world construction in language but a social, economic and political system of gradual subjugations and oppressions' in 'The will to choose or to reject' in Letty M. Russell (ed.), *Feminist Interpretation of the Bible*, Philadelphia: Westminster, 1995, p. 127.

11 Quoted by Linda Hogan in *From Women's Experience to Feminist Theology*, Sheffield: Sheffield Academic Press, 1995 (1964), p. 104.

12 *Changing the Subject: Women's Discourses and Feminist Theology*, Minneapolis: Fortress, 1994, p. 391.

13 *Changing the Subject*, p. 114.

14 Other groups that also felt unrepresented include South American and Asian women and lesbian theologians.

15 *White Women's Christ and Black Women's Jesus*, Atlanta: Scholars, 1989, p. 195.

16 Boston: South End, 1981. The initial quotation comes from Sojourner Truth's oft-quoted speech, made in the context of the struggle for emancipation from slavery.

17 Susan Thistlethwaite, *Sex, Race and God: Christian Feminism in Black and White*, New York: Crossroad, 1989, p. 44.

18 *Weaving the Visions: New Patterns in Feminist Spirituality*, San Francisco: Harper & Row, 1989, p. 3.

19 The whole passage goes: 'in its strong version postmodernism is committed to three theses: the death of man, understood as the death of the autonomous, self-reflective subject, capable of acting on principle; the death of history, understood as the severance of the epistemic interest in history of struggling groups in constructing their past narratives; the death of metaphysics, understood as the impossibility of criticising or legitimising institutions, practices, and traditions other than through the immanent appeal to the self-legitimation of "small narratives".' Seyla Benhabib, Judith Butler, Drucilla Cornell and Nancy Fraser, *Feminist Contentions: A Philosophical Exchange*, New York: Routledge, 1995, p. 49.

20 Fraser, *Feminist Contentions*, p. 71, emphasis as in original.

21 *Feminists Theorize the Political*, New York: Routledge, 1992, p. 26.

22 *Oneness*, Chapter 8.

23 *Formations of Class and Gender*, London: Sage, 1997, p. 167.

24 *Feminists Theorize the Political*, p. 38.

25 Words overheard at a local bus stop, spoken by a man probably in his sixties.

26 London: Sage, 1997.

27 *Formations of Class and Gender*, p. 15.

28 *Formations of Class and Gender*, p. 23.

29 Skeggs adopts here Pierre Bourdieu's typology of capital, though she is more interested in their affective nature than Bourdieu himself.

30 Minneapolis: Fortress, 1994.

2

BEYOND *BYKER GROVE*

This was a beautiful estate – this was called the Beverley Hills
estate. (Ivy, from St Justin's)

Walking around St Anthony's estate no longer calls to mind a place
where it is a pleasure and a privilege to live. The houses are not
unpleasant, being mainly Victorian red-brick terraces that are
often divided into 'Tyneside flats',[1] while the more recent buildings
include a small high-rise tower but predominantly continue the
terrace theme. The signs of deprivation lie elsewhere: in the litter,
which the strong east wind blows into even the best-kept gardens,
in the graffiti on the walls and the broken glass on the pavements,
in the number of houses empty and boarded up. The few shops
often keep their shutters down even when they are open, while
the goods they sell are basic, though not cheap.

Living in the vicarage, as in any of the surrounding houses, is
to be aware of a constant undercurrent of petty crime. Eggs or
rotten apples or half bricks often crash against the windows, cars
lose their hubcaps and gardens their furniture, while lads down
the pub are happy to supply you with the odd video or television, as long as you immediately forget where they came from.
This, though, is not the whole picture. The area may be rough but
it is 'canny rough'. There is very little street crime, so walking alone
after dark feels no more dangerous here than in any city area.
The broken glass on the streets does not include broken syringes
and there is little overt evidence of an ingrained drug culture,
although it cannot be denied that there are considerable numbers

of drug users on the estate. Among the gardens full of house-hold rubbish there are others that proudly display prize chrysan-themums or well-tended roses and honeysuckle. It is still possible to stop a vandal in his tracks by threatening to tell his mother, or grandmother, exactly what he is up to. St Anthony's may be a community under threat, but it is still, despite the odds, a community.

St Anthony's estate lies to the east of the city of Newcastle upon Tyne, bordering the river and forming part of the geographical area known as the Byker Basin. The estate grew out of the need to provide housing for the men working in the shipyards on the Tyne and its fortunes have declined along with those of the docks: 'We lost our heart really when we lost the shipbuilding' (Enid, from St Justin's). Many of the families are experiencing third-generation unemployment with no new opportunities in sight. It is often the women of the family who now find it easier to find paid work. The Geordie accent is a favourite with market researchers, which has encouraged a number of large call centres to settle in the North East. The work they offer is often part time, as is true for many of the jobs local women are able to get. Childcare is often shared out among the extended family, with aunts as well as grandmothers playing an essential role. It is also common to see fathers out with their young children and forming part of the group gathered around the school gates at home time.

One of the most obvious differences I noticed on moving from affluent Cambridge to deprived St Anthony's was the small number of cars parked in the streets. The two main modes of transport where we live now are foot and bus. The walk to the bus stop may involve an encounter with one of the local dogs, mainly good-tempered, who frequently roam the streets at will. In the queue, the older residents will greet each other by name, as will some of the younger ones. The talk is of family, problems with children or neighbours and, of course, the weather. Occasionally you will hear a comment on the failures of the local council or the government.

It is not surprising that local people should have such a view of the politicians in Westminster. Walker and Monkchester, which together make up the south part of the Byker Basin that contains St Anthony's, are, respectively, the thirtieth and thirty-first most deprived wards in England and Wales. There are still people who value the area, though, and would be unwilling to exchange it for a more affluent address:

And, um, you know as I say this has been our foundation and still is. People say why don't you move away, get a bungalow somewhere, but this is me – this is us, you know – and we just couldn't leave it. I love every inch of Walker, I do honestly. I just love it passionately. And you know you hear people pulling it down and I keep thinking, well, you don't know the good bits, you know. They haven't walked down the river and walked along right into the city, you know, they haven't seen the good people that are here. (Enid, from St Justin's)

There is a strong sense of local identity and local pride that prevents people from identifying themselves as deprived despite their poor material circumstances. This is still perceived by many as being a good place to live. Even the woman who said to me, 'I don't know how yous came to St Anthony's. You must have had hearts as big as lions', went on to say 'And yet there's worse places.'[2]

The racial make-up of St Anthony's has changed somewhat over the last few years. A little while ago it was extremely rare to see any but white faces on the street. The last wave of immigration that had a serious impact on the district was that of Irish labourers and their families in the nineteenth century. This partially explains the strength of the local Roman Catholic community. However, when the government decided to distribute asylum seekers more widely around the country, St Anthony's began to take on a more racially mixed appearance. This meant that there were, for the first time, noticeable – though still small – numbers of members of other races and faiths living on the estate. The impact was felt in St Aidan's Church of England Primary School, which went from having no children for whom English was not their first language to having children speaking Farsi, Arabic, Czech and Portuguese, among others.

The estate is currently in a state of flux, with no one entirely sure how it is going to change during the next decade. The council is looking at a programme of regeneration that will involve a certain amount of demolition and rebuilding. Questions have not yet been answered about the extent of this work and whether or not local families will be able to afford the new houses. Understandably, the process is the cause of much anxiety as well as a certain amount of hope. It is taking place within the context of consultations, but the local people are fairly sceptical about how much impact their opinions will have on the final decisions. Their worst scenario is to see the riverside yuppified, while local extended families are scattered by the rehousing process. The main hope is that new money will bring new life to the estate and return to it the respectability that many feel the area has lost.

The Walker/Byker area is served by five Anglican churches, three Roman Catholic, one Methodist and a free evangelical church. For this book, I selected three churches sited within ten minutes' walk of one another in the part of the area known as St Anthony's. These were St Aidan (Anglo-Catholic), St Justin (Roman Catholic) and Green Memorial Methodist Church. In order to prevent the study being heavily weighted in the Catholic direction, I added St Mark's (Anglican evangelical) to the list. This was the only church that did not fall into the St Anthony's area, but was close enough that the social and economic backgrounds of the congregation were the same. Members from each church knew members of the others and shared the facilities, or lack of them, that exist in the area. Another important reason for settling on these particular churches was their willingness to welcome me into their midst and the generosity of individual members of the churches in talking to me with great honesty about their spiritual lives.

It will become clear that St Aidan's is felt by its congregation to be a 'place of holiness' where there is access to a realm 'high above' with its inhabitants both holy and divine. These quotations come from a patronal anthem written for the church by its organist of many years who wanted to provide the congregation with a hymn that reflected their patron saint and showed their love for their church.

From the street, St Aidan's has a somewhat forbidding mien and on the outside does not look like a place that is held in great affection. It was built in 1868 at the command of Lord Northborne in order to provide for the spiritual needs of the men working in his shipyards on the Tyne. It is quite plain, of red brick, with no tower or steeple, continuing the same architectural feel as the red-brick terrace that shares its side of the street. It is modest while not being unattractive, but is spoilt by being surrounded by a high, spiked fence that has been painted black. Neither the vicar nor the congregation are happy with the defensive appearance this gives to the church, but fear the possible vandalism that might occur if it was not there. The church is particularly vulnerable as it is surrounded on two sides by a small public park. This land had been the churchyard, but was taken over by the council. The only remaining gravestones are those of a former vicar and his wife and daughter. The other side of the church not fronting the street is connected to a fairly modern church hall.

The gate in the church's fence is usually only unlocked for services. On a Sunday morning, the congregation enters through a dark porch to find an interior that is full of colour and interest. This is a matter of pride to the people of the church, one of the church wardens describing it as 'the most beautiful little church in Newcastle'. While this may reflect a certain amount of bias, St Aidan's certainly gives the impression of being cared for and valued, with the wood and brass lovingly cleaned and polished.

It is not a light church as the interior is the same brick as the outside, the windows provide more colour than light and the pews are dark wood. Like many of the local homes, there is a happy clutter of valued objects and, particularly, reminders of family – in this case, the family of saints. At the front on the north side is a statue of the patron saint; at the back on this side is one of St Laurence, which was rescued from a redundant local church; on the south there is St Joseph and also the Curé d'Ars who presides paternally over the small children's corner. On all sides there are statues of Mary: over the font, on the south front (with a votive candle stand that is better used than the patron saint's opposite), in the form of Our Lady of Walsingham and as part of the Holy Family. Altogether, the interior of the church proudly announces its Catholic identity.

The congregation, usually numbering around 30, gradually gathers in the 20 minutes or so before the main Sunday Eucharist, which is held at 9.30 a.m. Each new arrival greets most of the others already there and many will light a candle and stand in a moment of silent prayer before taking their accustomed seat. The overwhelming majority are female and over 50 – in fact, there are usually only 4 men present: the priest, the organist, a Sri Lankan refugee and the husband of one of the older women. There are more men at the quieter eight o'clock service – usually six out of the ten communicants. There may be three or four young children who have been brought along by their grandmothers. The dress is not very different from what is worn every day. Most of the congregation arrive on foot from the surrounding streets where they have lived all their lives. Only a handful come by bus and just one family by car.

The Eucharist at St Aidan's is, all in all, a solemn affair. It intentionally leaves space for each member of the congregation to focus on their individual devotions and emphasises the sacredness of the event taking place. There is a shared sense that this is truly a sacrament: a moment when God draws close and affirms 'his'[3] relationship with the worshippers.

The priest is the central figure in the carefully choreographed dance of the liturgy, but others also play a role. Members of the congregation read the lessons from the eagle lectern – peering round its imposing wings to make eye contact with the congregation – and also lead the intercessions. Some serve and there is a small choir to lead the singing. However, only the priest is allowed to administer the sacraments, both bread and wine. The service, which always includes incense and bells, is brought to a close with a final hymn and the singing of a canticle of Mary, after which the procession leaves, with many members of the congregation bowing to the priest as he passes by.

One or two of the congregation may leave immediately after the service – especially if Newcastle United are playing that Sunday. The rest gather in the hall next door for coffee and biscuits, sitting at tables with their particular friends. They will often chat for about 20 minutes, discussing family and health, sharing photographs and laughing together. The impression is of a real extended family, with all the support, cosiness and irritation that this implies. They will expect to see each other during the week and many will meet again on Wednesday evening for a mid-week Eucharist.

For many, even if they are only there on a Sunday, St Aidan's is a deeply loved and valued place to be. As Ann, one of my interviewees, put it, 'And I love that church down there, I absolutely love it ... I just absolutely love it. I can't express enough how much I love that church, I just love it.'

St Aidan's is proud of its Catholic heritage and would not dream of calling the priest anything other than 'Father'. This, and the tradition of bowing as he passes, would suggest that the power in the church rests with him. However, the reality is somewhat more complicated. From 1997–99 St Aidan's had an interregnum, during which the organist and his family – life-long members of the church – worked particularly hard to hold the church together and provide leadership. The almost iconic status of this family, as representative of the church's understanding of itself as traditional Northern Catholic, adds to their influence. This, combined with the current priest's reluctance to wield power unilaterally, dilutes the 'Father must be right' culture. It is also interesting to note that, in this traditional Catholic church, female voices are heard in every service and women are always robed and in the sanctuary. However, the final bar of ordination remains: only men can pass this barrier and, hence, only a man is holy enough to handle the consecrated elements.

There is a Church school that has close links with the parish. Many of the older women in the church attended it in the days when it was called 'Feed My Lambs'. It is now St Aidan's Church of England Primary School, with a roll of about 170 pupils. The parish priest is expected to take on the role of chair of governors and there are also two governors selected to represent the parochial church council. The school children come to church for a service once a term and Father Joseph takes regular assemblies. This means that the local children know who he is and will shout a greeting when they see him on the street. It is another way in which St Aidan's is deeply embedded in its local community.

The overall impression of St Aidan's is of a small and local congregation struggling to keep alive a dearly loved tradition. There are no para-church groups running on a regular basis, though there is a Lent group each year. The voices heard in the church all have a Geordie lilt, with the exception of the priest's. Its great strengths lie in its ability to nurture the spirituality of its members, support them in their daily lives and its witness to the local area of God's constant, loving presence. It also has a committed priest who is working to make the links to the local community more obvious and preserve all that is valuable in St Aidan's tradition while not allowing the church to just stand still. Its weaknesses lie in the very close-knit nature of the congregation, which can make it hard for newcomers to feel included, and in a sense of inertia among its ageing membership that makes change, however gentle, hard to implement.

It is interesting to compare the Anglo-Catholic St Aidan's with the Roman Catholic St Justin's. St Justin's is a young church in comparison – the parish was founded in 1951 and the church itself built in 1954. It was originally a daughter church of St Basil, Byker, and its founding reflects the upsurge in Roman Catholic attendance at mass following World War II. The parishes have only very recently been reattached, with one priest, Father Steven, now serving both churches. Father Steven had been in the post for about two years in 2000 when my study began, but left quite suddenly two years later, going back to his work as a nurse and leaving parochial ministry completely.

The church building forms part of a complex with St Justin's School,[4] which predates it by a few years, and the large presbytery. The noticeboard on the street has on it times for the services that are no longer accurate, but is in little danger of misleading people as it is mostly unreadable through the graffiti. There is, as seems traditional in the St Anthony's area, a high fence between the church and school grounds and the road, but the gate is usually open to allow access to the school. The church building itself looks older than its years, being built in traditional style in red brick.

It used to host a daily mass, but these have been reduced to Monday, Wednesday and Friday now that the priest has to look after St Basil's as well. The presence of St Justin's school strengthens the church in a number of ways. It is perceived to offer a better education than St Aidan's and some children are baptised into the church in order to ensure that they are given a place there. It also brings the church the services of a dedicated and exceptionally able religious, Sister Theresa, who contributes greatly to the church's Sunday school programme as well as being Headteacher of the school. She provides a consistency of leadership, offered with modesty and humour, while the parish priests come and go.

The Sunday mass takes place at 10.45 a.m., giving Father Steven time, just, to get there after the 9.30 a.m. mass at St Basil's. People begin to gather from about 10.20 a.m., most of them, like the congregation at St Aidan's, arriving on foot from the surrounding streets. They come in through an open door into a vestibule that is busy both with people, mainly women, standing and talking and tables bearing leaflets and books for the service. On the wall, there are photos of babies newly baptised at the church. The initial impression is one of bustle and liveliness, with children as well as adults flowing in to and out of the area. The chattiness continues in the church itself, with many people going to greet their friends before taking their seat in the pews. Some do come in more quietly and light a candle or kneel to pray in preparation for the service. By 10.45, there are about 60 to 70 adults scattered throughout the church, of whom 15 or so are men.

The space in which they sit is light and airy. The walls are painted cream and the many windows are plain glass – the only exception being the east windows, which have an abstract pattern in blues, greens and reds. The light wood pews are set on a red carpet and provide enough seating for at least 200 people. On the walls are Stations of the Cross carved into a similar light wood to that of the pews. The whole focus of the church is on the front, with an ornate altar of what looks like carved marble at the centre. The wall behind is painted a dark pink and a display of children's drawings forms a central arch against the background of beige tiles. The pictures consist of symbols representing the patriarchs and the members of the Holy Family. The decorations continue on the lectern, which has a copy of the head of Christ from the Turin Shroud attached to the front. There are statues on either side at the front. On the north side in the corner is St Theresa of Lisieux and, next to her, a Sacred Heart. These share a votive candle stand between them, while, above the Sacred Heart, hangs a large crucifix. On the opposite side, there hangs a large icon of the Virgin Mary with the Christ child and, beneath it, stands a small statue of the Virgin next to the font. It is a well-cared-for space, warm and pleasant to come in to.

The service begins with the singing of the first hymn as the procession enters. The singing, though accompanied by the organ, is somewhat reedy, but the procession is full of life as it consists of the Sunday school as well as the crucifer, acolytes and priest. The children are then sent over to the school and do not return until just before the Eucharistic prayer. This informal beginning

sets the mood for the service that follows, which is a straightforward parish mass. There is no mass book to follow as the expectation is that everyone there will know the service. Members of
the congregation, most often women, read the Old Testament and
Epistle and, later on, lead the intercessions.

Father Steven preaches the homily without notes, talking very
directly to the congregation. The first sermon I heard there was
based on the text 'Blessed are the poor'. Father Steven contrasted
the values of the world and the Church, telling us that it is God,
not money, that brings happiness and that we, as Christians, should
live lives that are different from those of our non-Christian neighbours. In his insistence on not speaking evil of others and guarding
against forming cliques within the congregation, there was a sense
that he was addressing particular problems he perceived at
St Justin's.

When the children return after the Offertory, they take their
work to the altar rail and then return to their seats, staying for
the Eucharistic prayer as the mass moves towards the receiving of
Communion. This is the pivotal moment for many in the congregation, as Marie, a convert to Roman Catholicism, put it very
succinctly: 'The best thing about church is the body and blood –
that's what I mainly go to church for, to receive.'

In the other churches in my study, I had automatically joined
in receiving with the rest of the congregation. The situation was
different at St Justin's as I knew Father Steven would not give
Communion to an Anglican. Feeling uncomfortable staying in the
pew, though I would not have been the only one, the second time
I was there I decided that I would go up to receive a blessing. It
felt uncomfortable being excluded from Communion, so uncomfortable that it unexpectedly brought tears to my eyes. Some people
left immediately they had received, but the majority waited for the
final hymn and then chatted as they quite quickly left the building.
There was no coffee after the service, but Father Steven and Sister
Theresa did try to greet people on their way out.

It may look to outsiders, and to some of the congregation, that power at St Justin's is firmly in the hands of the priest. There are no bodies within the congregation that he has to consult when making decisions, although there are diocesan guidelines to follow. However, Father Steven himself sees things somewhat differently. He talks of there being something of a 'power struggle' for him at St Justin's as he tries to assert his own will over those of the established leaders in the congregation, particularly the Women's Guild. Although accepting that he is called to serve, he does not believe that this means he is called to be the congregation's servant and feels strongly that the priest should be listened to on matters of doctrine and ethical teaching. He would like to see members of the congregation growing in confidence and spiritual maturity so that they can help the church reach out to the local community. A large part of his ministry is spent with the unchurched and his shaven head and tattoos, along with his Geordie accent, make him an approachable figure in this working-class parish.

The women of St Justin's, like the women of St Aidan's, speak about their church as being a place where it is possible to feel closer to God. The more informal style of the service does not translate into a lower regard for the sanctity of the sacrament, nor, perhaps surprisingly, does it seem to have impacted on the individualistic understanding of the central purpose of worship. The priest may delight in having so many children present, but, for many of the older women, their noise is resented as it detracts from their personal concentration on the presence of God in the sacraments.

The main midweek activity of St Justin's, apart from the weekday masses, is the rosary group, which meets in the local sheltered accommodation on a Wednesday evenings. It has about 15 members, including 2 men who come occasionally. Easy chairs and sofas are set in a circle around a table on which is set a statue of the Virgin Mary, encircled by a large wooden rosary and flanked by two candles.

When everyone is settled, the evening begins with a short rosary for peace. Before the main rosary, requests for prayers are invited

and most members mention names, occasionally with an explanation of the need. Five decades of the rosary are then said, with
a different leader for each decade. People handle their beads with
the ease of long familiarity. After a recitation of the Walsingham
liturgy, and prayers for the conversion of England, the formal part
of the evening finishes with a hymn. The first night I was present,
this was 'Mary I love you', by an unknown author, sung to the
tune of 'Annie's Song', of which a typical verse goes:

Mary I love you – your constant prayers for me
Enrich every blessing – given anew
With love do I give you,
My life now and always
Each beat of my heart is – a love song for you.

Susan, the leader of the group, told me at the end of the hour-long
session what a powerful tool of prayer the rosary is. It obviously
has a powerful attraction for the members of the group, who pray
with great concentration and talk together afterwards with much
affection. I was struck by the sense they have of important work
being done by their meeting together to pray and felt that, for
most, though not all, the prayer is more important than the social
side of the evening. If I am honest, the atmosphere was a little
piously emotional for my taste. The room was, in the tradition of
residential homes for the elderly, somewhat overheated and, to me,
so was some of the sentimental language directed at Mary. I was
surprised to feel this way, having expected to find a group devoted
to prayer with a female focus an uplifting, rather than cloying,
experience.

St Justin's has the highest attendance figures of the four churches
in the study. It benefits from its close links to the school, which
is more popular than the Church of England primary school at
St Aidan's. However, both the priest and the congregation are
finding the new link with St Basil's hard going and there is some
tension between the way in which the priest sees his role and how

his laity envisions it. There is an awareness that links with the local community need to be strengthened – in particular, that the church needs to offer more for the different disadvantaged groups it is not yet reaching. St Justin's future existence seems secure for the next few years at least. The challenge it faces is deciding how introverted or extroverted that future is going to be.

The most visible church building in the St Anthony's area is Green Memorial Methodist Church, though to many people it is not readily identifiable as a church. It stands on Walker Road, the main road through the estate, on land formerly occupied by St Aidan's original church hall. The foundation stone of the building was laid in March 1976, with the intention of providing a new home for St Anthony's Methodist Church, which had been compulsorily purchased by the council, and for Green Memorial Chapel, which was sited about a mile and a half away. It is a large, square, brick building with a rather strange triangular grey-slate roof, surrounded by grass and, like St Aidan's, a high, black, spiked fence. These railings are a source of dismay to the minister, Reverend Patricia West, who feels that they separate the church and the community into two different camps: 'So I think, yes, my ultimate hope is that the church – and by that I mean both the building and the people – become more part, an accepted part, of the community. And while those railings are round it I don't think that will happen.'

The interior of the church is divided into two main spaces – a worship area and a hall – as well as containing a kitchen and a couple of offices. On entering the church for a Sunday service, the visitor is usually greeted in the lobby and directed through the door to the left. This leads into the worship area, a carpeted room in which the windows are in the roof, letting in some light but providing no view of the outside. Rows of wooden chairs, which could seat up to a hundred people, face a raised dais on which there are a lectern, an altar table and a font with a flower stand in front of it. In the wall behind, a large cross stands proud of the surrounding brickwork and two banners hang on either side – one illustrating the 'Spirit of God' and the other 'Peace'. The remaining decoration consists of a banner for the Girls' Brigade and two back-lit stained-glass panels dating from the late nineteenth century and dedicated to members of the original congregations. One illustrates the good works of Dorcas, while the other shows Jesus welcoming the children. The overall impression is of a plain room with a few touches that personalise it and mark it out as a space for worship.

The congregation gathers chattily in the final few minutes before the service begins. It usually numbers between 20 and 30, with a large proportion attending both the morning and evening services. There are about seven or eight men who come regularly and a couple of children may be there in the morning. Unlike both St Aidan's and St Justin's, quite a large proportion of the congregation come by car or bus.[5] The room still feels quite empty when everyone is gathered, with people sitting two or three to a row.

The minister, lay or ordained, leading the service enters by a side door, usually dressed in smart but ordinary clothes, and begins the service with a 'good morning' or a 'good evening' from the lectern. What follows in the rest of the service depends greatly on the style and preference of the worship leader. There will usually be five hymns, accompanied on the electric organ, two or more Bible readings, some intercessory prayers and a sermon. There might also be a children's talk, a confession, a modern reading or psalm. The leader's may be the only voice that is heard or they may ask a member of the congregation to do one of the readings or the prayers. More than any of the other churches, the quality of the worship experience depends on the expertise of the person leading it. At its best, it can be challenging, innovative and thoughtful; at its worst it can be bland and unengaging.

The services are usually non-Eucharistic, but there is Communion about twice a quarter. One of these services always coincides with the Covenant Service, which takes place on the first Sunday of each year. This includes one of the most powerful parts of Methodist worship, the covenant prayer, in which every member is invited to recommit themselves and all their life to God. The attendance at this service rivals that at the main festivals of Christmas and Easter and is an integral part of the Christian year for Green Memorial's faithful.

Most members of the congregation stay on at the end of the service for a cup of tea and a chat in the hall across the corridor. Like St Aidan's, there is a sense of a small group who know each other well and are genuinely concerned for each other's well-being. They may be a little shy about talking to visitors, but there is always a smile and a sense that your presence is a welcome addition rather than an intrusion. The congregation may meet each other during the week, either as helpers at the Junior Youth Club or Girl's Brigade or as members of the Green Memorial Singers[6] or the Family Meeting Point. They might also go along to events hosted elsewhere on the circuit, but, like most congregations, are often reluctant to move outside the confines of their own church building.

The Family Meeting Point was suggested to me as a good place to meet some of the women who have been most closely involved with the life of the church over many decades. The title is somewhat misleading as the meeting consists not of families, but a group of between 8 and 12 older women. I was immediately aware of being both the youngest, and the tallest, woman there, but was warmly welcomed into the circle.

The women made sure that I was introduced to the group's leader, a lady in her eighties who, despite being bent almost double and only able to look down, was still very much in charge. She introduced each session, which began with hymns sung unaccompanied, but enthusiastically, and prayers, which always included the names of any members who were ill. The bulk of the meeting consisted of a talk given by an invited speaker, usually a woman, and most often one of the licensed ministers of the circuit. These included a parable of the Christian life based on weaving, with a practical demonstration, lessons for Christian life drawn from tea towels (both of these by the new minister, Patricia) and a consideration of the atonement (by the church's community worker). The emphasis was on strengthening daily Christian living and affirming the centrality of God's love.[7]

After the talk, there was tea and the exchange of news, which focused particularly on the state of people's health, especially of those who were not able to make the meeting. The regular members were warm and bantered with one another, giving the sense of a group who knew each other well and were well used to tolerating each other's weaknesses. When one of the long-standing members died, there was no great outpouring of grief, but a quiet sharing of sorrow at their loss. They were not particularly interested in the world outside, which rarely got a mention in the prayers, but rather in supporting one another through the daily business of life. I felt not so much an intruder as an irrelevance in the group, whose strength lay in the length of time that these women had journeyed together. It was like touching briefly on the outskirts of a family who, whatever their little irritations with one another, are united at heart.

Green Memorial Methodist Church judges itself a success in the way that it has managed to integrate two very different congregations. However, along with most of the other local churches, it is now feeling the effect of an ageing and shrinking congregation. The individuals who used to be a powerful influence on the life of the church no longer have the health and energy to play such a major role. Some of the slack is being taken up by the church community worker, who provides a focus for new initiatives, especially where these foster links with the surrounding area.[8] However, it must be said that many of the congregation see the surrounding streets as a place of threat rather than a potential source of new members and the high fence as a barrier they value for keeping their cars and their church building safe from vandalism. Patricia West, the new minister, is attempting to encourage the congregation to look beyond the church walls, both in social mission and evangelism. It has yet to be seen what impact her ministry will have.

Joining in the worship at Green Memorial Methodist is a very easy thing to do: there are no books to follow, apart from the hymnal, and no ritual gestures to learn. This makes the visitor immediately comfortable. The members of the congregation are faithful and committed, but it might be fair to say that their focus is primarily on the past rather than the future. They look back to a time when the Sunday school was full, the members were spread more evenly over a range of ages and they had more energy to take on new initiatives. However, this is not true of all the members and there are those who see their mission as bringing new life to the surrounding area rather than just preserving the existing life of the church. Interestingly, this church had the fewest regular roles in services for members of the congregation. This may have contributed to their reluctance to talk to me about their faith as they were not used to hearing their voices in this context or contributing individually to the chorus of faith. Their voices were heard, but they expressed their faith within the context of responses and, particularly, hymns, where they spoke as a group with the support of other voices all around.

Green Memorial Methodist is still a place that offers companion-ship and the reassurance of the familiar to its members and – something that is not to be underestimated – provides a place where their voices can share in the old hymns together. Like the other local churches, it is finding it hard to reach out and bring new members in. If I found the worship experience there to be sometimes bland, that probably has as much to say about my Anglican preference for ritual as it does about the experience itself.

The furthest church from my house is St Mark's, which thinks of itself as the parish church of Byker, though the area is actually shared with another Anglican church, St Leonard's. When I began my research, St Mark's was in the third year of an interregnum. The church was kept going by the efforts of a small group of women who made up the bulk of the parochial church council and included both church wardens. They were assisted by the Rural Dean of the East End Deanery, whose often difficult job it was to find priests to preside at the weekly Sunday Eucharist. The Diocese was keen to fill the vacancy and invited a number of priests to consider the post, but without success. The reasons for this failure soon became apparent.

St Mark's was built in the middle years of the nineteenth century and dedicated in 1860. It sits, with the vicarage, the church hall and a verger's house, in a long-extinct quarry near the top of a hill. The site is steeply walled on two sides and falls away sharply on the other two. The Byker wall has been built around it to replace the Victorian terraces that used to be there. Unfortunately, the site has been the source of many problems. The church hall, built in the 1970s, is unusable as the cliff under it is subsiding. The vicarage, also dating from the 1970s, is considered unsuitable because of its isolation. The church, therefore, is surrounded by empty and useless buildings and, with no houses overlooking the area, has become a prime site for vandalism and drug abuse.

Entering the church for the first time one Sunday morning, I was immediately struck by its extreme dereliction. The lights shining out of the windows were the only sign that the church was still in use and it took me two attempts to open the heavy inner door. This is reached through a completely dark porch, which is daunting and very unwelcoming. The church is a large building, intended to house the hundreds of local labourers whom the Victorians optimistically hoped would attend. It has a high, vaulted roof, painted red in the nave and green in the chancel. Apart from this, there is little colour. The large windows are plain glass, which in many places has been broken, with even the leads bent out of shape (they are now covered with a protective layer of polycarbonate sheeting). The pews are dark wood, there are grey stone pillars and the walls are cream plaster. All over these walls, there are patches of mould and cracks in the plasterwork. This evidence of damp is reinforced by buckets strategically placed over the floor and tea towels protecting some of the reading desks. Heating is provided by electric radiators suspended from the roof, but these did very little to pierce the extreme cold of the January Sundays that I was there. However, against this picture of decay must be set the emotional attachment that is still felt for this dilapidated church. In the words of Angela, a member of St Mark's for many years:

It's, um, for all, for me the feeling is still there. The feeling of God's presence the minute you walk in, I know God's with us all the time, but, you know, God's presence is there. You know the feeling that when you go in he's there, and welcoming you in and encouraging you, strengthening you to go on. Um, it has changed and unfortunately at the minute it is obviously at its worst its ever been. It's sad. It is sad.

Just inside the doorway there is a small table set with the books for the service. The congregation arrive in the last ten minutes or so before the service starts, collect their books and take their seats in the choir stalls up in the chancel. There are 12 who regularly attend, of whom 2 are men, and all are over 50, with most being well over 60. Although St Mark's characterises itself as evangelical, the worship is quite traditional. They still use the Alternative Service Book (ASB)[9] and have a weekly Eucharist, the style of which may vary slightly with each visiting priest, but is usually spoken. They may sing choruses as well as hymns, with an enthusiasm that helps to make up for the lack of musical accompaniment, but the style of the service is reverent and thoughtful. This is felt to be important by some of the remaining members. To quote Angela:

I think the Eucharist is very, very important. And I think it's also very, very important that the Eucharist is kept as a dedicated, reverent, respectful service. I think, yes, I'm quite happy with a prayer and praise – I can sing hymns and clap along and what have you, in the right setting – but I don't think that sort of thing should be part of the Eucharist.

The placing of the congregation in the choir stalls right next to the simple altar allows for an intimate atmosphere. One of the women will walk to the lectern to do the readings, another will lead the intercessions from her place in the pews and another will take the collection. The priest distributes both the bread and the wine. This is not, as at St Aidan's, because there would be a problem with a lay person doing so, but because the limited numbers make it unnecessary. At the end of the service, Constance, the registered lay worker, will collect the sacrament for a midweek service at her flat. There is no coffee after the service, because of the lack of a church hall, and the members of the congregation slowly make their way out, chatting to one another as they go.

The group of women who perform the different tasks during the service meet every Monday evening for a Bible study and planning session. This takes place in the house of one of the churchwardens, who lives just a couple of minutes from the church. There are three core members (two of whom are sisters) who will attend without fail, unless they are away, and three or four others who come quite regularly. I was welcomed as an occasional visitor to the group, which, it should be said, is not intentionally women only but has become that way due to the shortage of men at St Mark's. I came to greatly admire the commitment and humour of these women as they struggled to keep their church alive and face an uncertain future.

The group worked through different books of the Bible, with members taking it in turns to lead a session – usually with the help of a study guide. They did not shirk the less well-known books – indeed, during the first two sessions I attended they were studying Ezra. Each brought their own Bible and they sat around the dining room table drinking coffee and deciphering the message that the text held for them as a church and as individuals. Although, as with any group, there were those who spoke more often than others, they all contributed and each was listened to with respect. There was a great deal of laughter, especially when individuals felt that their own weaknesses were being highlighted in what they were reading, but underlying all was a serious feeling that this was important work for strengthening their Christian understanding and safeguarding the faith of the Church.

It must be said that I was not always comfortable with the lessons that the group found within the pages of the Old Testament. They read with a belief in the historical truth of the account and a conviction that its message can be simply transferred to contemporary situations. In Ezra, for example, they identified completely with the beleaguered people of God surrounded by the hordes of the ungodly. They drew strength from the thought that the Jews had had to wait many years before their temple was completed, reassuring themselves that a three-year interregnum did not mean that they had been deserted by God. They also felt that they were the people of God awash in a sea of pagan unbelief and roundly condemned much of contemporary culture and the ethics of their neighbours. This condemnation was leavened with an awareness of their own sins and shortcomings and their re-minder to one another that Christians should not be judgemental. The overall impression, nonetheless, was that they were the direct heirs of the covenant, who were in a privileged spiritual and ethical position vis-à-vis the bulk of their community.

The group who meet for Bible study end their session by plan-ning the hymns for the next week's service, allocating readings and intercessions and often discussing the possible future of the church. There is an awareness of the difficulties that they face and that, even if a new priest is appointed, things will have to change. Their vision for the future includes hopes for the church building itself:[10]

> I'd like to see us end up with a building that we can manage. A building that will welcome people as the church welcomes people now. A building that people will want to come into, but for the right reasons. I think we need to be sure, very sure, people recog-nise that it is a church – regardless of what is built into it. (Angela)

and for the people who might be attracted to come:

I'd like to see a church with people in who have a heart, a real heart, for Jesus. Because I think that is, that's the key, you know, because that's where everything starts – with Jesus in the church, you know. (Jane, a member of St Mark's for 20 years)

There is a real danger that St Mark's might close unless this vision becomes closer to being a reality. The congregation is fighting for its survival and feeling the effort of this. The fact is, 12 ageing members, however faithful and committed, have an uphill struggle to make St Mark's a going concern once again.

(Postscript: The situation at St Mark's has changed somewhat during the timespan of this study. It has now been included with another parish, St Matthew's, and shares their priest in charge. The Diocese is still considering how the church can move forwards, with the help of the priest in charge and a church development officer specialising in working with the Church in areas of urban decline. It is now less likely that the church building will be redeveloped, so alternative venues are being explored. The congregation is not enthusiastic about only having a part-time incumbent, but realistic and accepts that this is the most that can be expected in the present circumstances.)

It is impossible to understand the individuals whose experiences form the basis of this book without grasping something of the society in which their experiences, and their selves, were formed. My view is necessarily that of an outsider, despite the fact that I now live in the heart of the estate. I am not 'at home' here – neither in the estate as a whole nor in the congregations being studied – so the area will not have the same appearance for me as it does for the local women and I can only hope to catch part of what it means to, and for, them.

St Anthony's estate is not the easiest, nor the most comfortable, of places to live, yet it is not a place that established families want to escape from. Their hopes are focused less on achieving a bungalow in a 'better' part of town than on seeing St Anthony's return to the working community that they remember from their childhood. This may be an unrealistic hope, perhaps based on idealised memories, but it expresses the loyalty that is still felt towards the estate and the deep rootedness of the women who have lived there all their lives. 'Home' for them is not somewhere that you carry with you around the country, but a particular location where your memories, and your family, establish you as part of a distinct community. Moving out of the area can mean something approaching exile, as it did for Catherine, from St Mark's:

> We moved to the Midlands for about seven years. I hated it . . . Leicester. Oh, I enjoyed it while I was there, but I hated being away from here. I hated being away from the family, um, people I'd grown up with . . . they didn't seem to have that welcoming . . . Because mainly the people we did socialise with were exiled Geordies.

The self-identity of the women interviewed is communal as well as individual: they know themselves as part of the local community as well as separate individuals within it. This has both positive and negative implications. On the positive side, it means that they are surrounded by relationships, avoiding the danger of alienation and isolation that is supposed to mark modern life. They know who they are because they are known by their family and their neighbours. On the negative side, it means that they identify closely with the reputation of the local area, too, and so feel marginalised and powerless within the wider society. They are held static within a web of interconnecting duties and attachments that provide a rich depth to relationships, but also inhibit transformative change. Understanding the implications of this style of society for the spiritual experiences of the women of the estate is an important part of this book.

The churches the women attend also have a profound effect on their understanding of their faith and their place within the faith community. The strength of their attachment to their particular church cannot be doubted: the language that they use speaks of 'love' and 'lovely', of being in God's presence in a special way when they are within the church walls. These feelings have, for the majority of the women, come out of many years spent worshipping within one place, which has allowed them to build up a rich deposit of memories and associations attached to it. Although they may experience other churches when they go to the ecumenical services arranged in the area or by their involvement in the charismatic movement, their loyalty is firmly fixed to their particular denomination and their own churchmanship within that denomination. Having said that, three of the Roman Catholic women had originally been brought up Protestant, but became Roman Catholic as a result of marrying Roman Catholic men. They all date their involvement with their church from this point on.

In only one of the churches – Green Memorial Methodist – do the women have the chance to experience a woman minister in charge of the church. In the other three, such a situation would be felt by some of each congregation to militate against the revealed will of God for the relationship between men and women. This point is explored in some detail in Chapter 5. In St Justin's, there is a role model for female leadership in Sister Theresa, the Headteacher of the school, but all sacramental authority still rests in the hands of a man. Even more strangely, it is at St Mark's – where the church has effectively been run by a group of women for the last three years – that the objections to women's leadership are most endemic. There does not seem to be any change in theology and faith in Green Memorial Methodist to reflect the gender change in leadership – no more acceptance of female language and imagery for God than elsewhere – and the women were the least comfortable while talking about their beliefs.

The experience of worship is very different in each of the churches and, presumably, has also differed considerably over the years with changes in clergy and authorised liturgy. However, the experience for most of the women is one of continuity rather than change, traditions warmly upheld and innovations questioned. Edith, from St Aidan's, is extreme rather than atypical in her statement:

> Well, I can't really tell you much, except there's nobody can change my faith, nobody can change my church. I'm sorry about all this that's going on now, but I don't bother about it. They can change what they like, but I just say the same old thing, do the same old thing.

Church provides continuity and the comfort of the familiar rather than being valued as a place of challenge and transformation. Worship follows well-known patterns and brings together a well-known group of people. In most cases, members of the congregation play a considerable part in producing the worship that they enjoy – by reading, serving, leading intercessions, decorating the church for different festivals – but they do not have ultimate control over what is offered to them. Most are content with this structure, though there are some – notably at St Marks – who feel that they do too much and a few others who feel that they would like to do more.

The women spoke fondly of past priests and ministers and positively, but more critically, about the present incumbents. They obviously felt that they have an impact on the life of the church, which is gilded with hindsight and more judgemental in the here and now. The easiest church in which to worship as a newcomer was Green Memorial Methodist, with its informal liturgy and few demands for congregational participation beyond the singing of hymns. St Mark's was very welcoming, but, with so few members, also exposing, with the added challenge of singing in a small group without instrumental accompaniment. St Aidan's was welcoming to me as the vicar's wife, but quite demanding in the liturgical moves that the congregation needed to know. St Justin's – having no book to help you join in with the rest of the congregation – was the hardest work for the new attender. However, while none of the churches is thriving in numerical terms, it is St Justin's that has the largest congregation and includes most children and younger people.

The faith and spirituality of the women will be seen to be intimately connected with their church life. They are not of the type who see their belief as something that is fundamentally private: their relationship with God is, as will become apparent, intensely personal, but it is experienced within their membership of a believing community, as well as a geographical community. The formative influence that their respective churches have had on the spirituality of the individual women will also become apparent in each of the successive chapters, while in Chapter 5 their own view of the Church will be considered in some detail. The women are not like characters playing their individual roles against the backdrop of their local society. That they have become who they are is, partially at least, a result of the social and spiritual spaces in which they have lived their lives. It is the resulting theology and spirituality – both rich, both limited – that will now be explored.

Notes

1 These flats have separate front doors: one leading into the ground floor flat and the other opening on to stairs up to the first floor flat. Typically the back yard faces the back yard of the next street with a narrow alleyway running between them.

2 Sarah, a member of St Aidan's in her sixties.

3 God will usually be referred to with male pronouns throughout this book as this is the way that the women speak of God. The quotation marks here indicate that this language is not comfortable for me.

4 A Roman Catholic primary school, taking children from ages 5 to 11.

5 This is largely because of the wide geographical area covered by the two original churches.

6 A group that finally came to an end during the time of my research as the members were becoming too elderly to cope with the demands of singing at concerts.

7 Later on in my time at St Anthony's, I was invited to lead one of the sessions, which I did. I was also asked to lead the Girls' Brigade

as they desperately needed a younger woman to take this on. I had to decline.

8 For example, suggesting the church premises as a venue for a drama production on domestic violence organised by the East End Women's Forum.

9 The Alternative Service Book (ASB) was officially superseded in the Church of England by Common Worship in 2000, but its continued use was permitted in churches where there was an interregnum.

10 The Diocese and the parish are considering the possibilities of re-developing the building with a local housing association. This would mean that the chancel area would become the church and the nave would be developed into flats. The problems with the scheme are not a lack of enthusiasm from the congregation of St Mark's, but the difficulty of raising the necessary funds.

3

'EE – YOU'RE JUST
LIKE GOD'

ELLEN: If you think about God, do you have any picture in your
mind?

EDITH: Well, the main one usually when I think about him, I
always like to think of him like this. He is right up in
the heavens somewhere, you know, a great big man all
in white things, grey hair and white beard. Very benign.
There's a – there's a Pope in Rome Cathedral, I can't
remember his name. Big hefty man he was ... And he
was really nice. I always picture God like that.

This is an image of God calculated to create horror in the minds
of contemporary theologians, especially those who have been at
all influenced by feminism. Edith's image of God – in which distant
divine power and distant male ecclesiastical power clearly reflect
one another – is the exact opposite of the images of the divine
that many contemporary theologians embrace. Here in a nutshell
is the dilemma that runs throughout this book: how to honour
the lived experience of the working-class women in the pews while
also holding on to the best theological insights of the academy.[1]

In order to try to achieve mutual respect, this chapter sets the
experiences of the interviewees alongside models of God from
the academy, as well as setting the insights of academic theology,
especially feminist theology, alongside the experiences of the interviewees. We will look at both images of God and the language
used about God by the women interviewed. This will take the

question 'Who is God?' further for the women who attend church in the East End of Newcastle and help us to see how such images work as a liberative or oppressive force within their spirituality and their wider lives. We will also see how far, if at all, the images of God from the pews can be brought together with those from the academy to begin to create a 'choral theology' of the Church as a whole.

One of the central concerns that feminist theology has brought to the academy, and which has been widely embraced, is the need to move away from talking about God as if God were male. If not all would go so far as to say with Mary Daly that, 'If God is male, then the male is God', she certainly expresses a concern here that is at the heart of feminist theological writing. This can be seen in the work of Christian feminist theologians as well as in that of Jewish and Buddhist writers and, of course, in post-Christian feminism.[2] In the Christian context such work offers the Church an opportunity to address an imbalance in its theological thinking and to recognise anew that all its members are created in the image of God.

The motivation for this work in the academy is two-fold, and which element has priority will differ from one theologian to the next. The first part lies in the implications of the quotation given above – 'If God is male, then the male is God.' Feminist theologians point out that the elevation of male status above female, if not caused by, has at least been bolstered by religions in which the divine and the male are shown as linked. While none of the world's major religions actually teaches that God is male – Christianity, for example, insisting that God is beyond and other than both human genders – there is still a supposed connection between divinity and masculinity. Within Christianity, God is 'King', 'Lord' and 'Father' rather than 'Queen', 'Lady' and 'Mother'. It is thought appropriate to use the male pronoun when referring to God and adopt images such as God as shepherd rather than God as house-wife, even though both occur together within Luke's Gospel.[3]

There is not room here to explore the full implications that such a connection between God and men has had for women within the Church over the centuries. However, it would be hard for anyone to deny that it has contributed to an inequality of power between the sexes, an inequality that can still be seen within the hierarchical structures of many of the world's largest denominations. Rosemary Radford Ruether is not alone in pointing out that God, men, the intellect and the spiritual are routinely placed at the positive pole of a dualism that has at its negative pole the earthly, women, emotions and the body. The hope for feminist theologians is that, in ending the monopoly of male images and language for God, there will also be an end, or the beginning of an end, of the devaluation of women within the Church and beyond.

This is an ethical motivation for theological rethinking in which the quest for justice is paramount and the quest for truth, while not ignored, is in second place. This may sound strange to those who are used to thinking of theology as, above all, an undertaking to enquire into the truth about God. However, theology has always also been concerned with the right ordering of human affairs in relation to God or, to put it in other words, with the way in which human beings should live in order to embody the will of God on Earth. It is this strand of theological endeavour that these feminist theologians have inherited, and expanded on, in their concern for just social relationships in the here and now.

The second motivation, however, is, located in the heart of the quest for truth. The focus here is on discerning, as far as is possible, the true nature of God. Rather than concentrating on the implications of male pictures of God for the relationship between the sexes, interest centres on exploring who God is in Godself.

In Christian theology, a justification for widening images of God to include the female can be found in the story of creation that begins the Bible: 'So God created humankind in his image, in the image of God he created them; male and female he created them'.[4] In other words, both women *and* men are made in the image of God and, therefore, both male and female imagery can be appropriately used when speaking of God or, at least, it is as appropriate as any purely human language and imagery can ever hope to be. The argument here is that omitting female imagery for God leaves us with a hopelessly lopsided view of who God is, so limiting both our understanding of God and our ability to relate fully to God. The justice that is at stake here is not equality of the sexes, but the need to do justice, as far as our limited human capacity allows, to the reality of God.

The ways in which feminist theologians use female imagery for God are strikingly diverse. In some cases, the image of the Goddess entirely replaces that of God and no male language for God is retained. This can be seen particularly vividly in the work of the American theologian[5] Carol Christ. The majority of feminist theologians do not take their work of reconstruction so far. Preferring to stay within their faith traditions, they work to supplement, rather than replace, male language for God. In some cases, this means searching the Bible to find previously overlooked female images for God, like the one in Luke's parables referred to above. In others, it means finding new ways to speak about God that, nonetheless, remain true to the image of God revealed in the faith's foundation documents and ongoing tradition. Within Christianity, this would mean remaining true to the image of God revealed in Jesus Christ and attested to in the Bible and Church tradition. Rather than wanting to see male language for God disappear, they hope for a Church where it is considered appropriate to address God as both 'he' and 'she' and where men and women will be believed to be of equal standing in the eyes of God and so of one another.

Before looking at the images of God in the lives of the women of St Anthony's, I want to introduce two portraits of God from two women of the academy. Their pictures will provide a counterpoint both to the portraits of God painted by the words of the women interviewed and the images of God offered by the parishes in this study. The two academics are Luce Irigaray, a French feminist, and Grace Jantzen, a feminist philosopher of religion based in the UK.

Luce Irigaray's religious ideas are based on the need she perceives for there to be a female divine genealogy to set alongside the male divine genealogy. The clearest way in which to explain this lies in her suggestion that every woman ought to have on her bedroom wall an icon of St Anne with the Blessed Virgin Mary. In other words, Irigaray's portrait of God is one in which mothers and daughters, rather than fathers and sons, take centre stage. Not that she sees a need to get rid of the Father and Son, but, rather, supplement them so that there are female images for women to aspire to as well as male ones for men. Such a portrait of God would give women a transcendental goal to aim at and a transcendental standard to measure themselves against: 'We have no female Trinity. But as long as woman lacks a divine made in her image she cannot establish her subjectivity or achieve a goal of her own. She lacks an ideal that would become her goal or path in becoming.'[6] This would mean that women would no longer have to measure themselves competitively against each other, nor attempt to deny their nature by competing on male criteria. The current situation – where there is only a male image of divinity – is seen as cramping women's possible growth and limiting their hope of finding their own true identity. In her own words, 'Now that women are today, orphaned, without she-gods, goddesses, a divine mother of daughters, without a spiritual genealogy, they will do anything to assert a degree of independence, risking a further loss of female identity.'[7]

Irigaray's argument is taken up and extended by Grace Jantzen in her book proposing a new feminist philosophy of religion entitled *Becoming Divine*. Jantzen's intention is to challenge the preoccupation in philosophy of religion with whether or not God exists and, instead, to call our attention to what human beings would be like if they reached for the divine in themselves:

> But what if we take seriously the idea . . . that the goal of religion is becoming divine? With that as a goal, the truth question recedes in importance. If human characteristics are projected on to the divine, if humans seek to *become* divine, the important question will not be so much one of truth as one of adequacy.[8]

It is in the area of adequacy – particularly with regard to women – that Jantzen follows Irigaray in her criticisms of traditional Christianity. Both writers (along with many other feminist philosophers and theologians) characterise Christianity as being focused on the transcendent, the other-wordly, to the detriment of the this-worldly, and as providing a divine ideal that only suits men.

In order to keep the focus on this world, Jantzen hopes to replace the idea of salvation with the idea of flourishing. In other words, rather than concentrating on a Saviour who arrives from elsewhere to rescue us, we would work for a world where we all help one another to flourish and grow in fulfilment. Instead of a God who provides 'his' people with a 'knight in shining armour' we have a God who is present in the world itself: 'incarnated within us and between us.'[9] Think St Francis and St Clare rather than St George.

Jantzen is very clear that this new divine image must be more than 'God in a skirt'. In other words, it is not enough to change God's gender while keeping the belief that God is a transcendent and disembodied spirit. In order to demolish the old dualism – in which the spiritual is valued above the material, and women and the material are identified with one another – Jantzen feels the need for a more dramatic change. In fact, she proposes a pantheist theology, in which God and the world are to be identified with one another. The material can no longer be downvalued as there is no separate spiritual realm – God, and everything else, is only present in matter – so the dualism is demolished and women are rescued from their subordinate status. The other benefit of her theology lies in its potential to keep our focus on this world as the site of all truth and value, preventing traditional religion's flight to other worlds: 'Now if we take instead a pantheistic symbolic in which that which is divine precisely *is* the world and its ceaselessly shifting bodies and signifiers, then it is this which must be of ultimate value.'[10]

Grace Jantzen's new philosophy of religion is not intended to spring from her own imagination and intellect alone, but from what she calls a 'trustworthy community'. Her aim is to reflect the reality of women's lives in her rethinking of God and she is critical of other feminist writers who, she feels, have not taken this on board and so have failed to break far enough away from conventional thinking: 'It is not at all obvious that a concept of God genuinely derived from imaginative thinking from women's lives (especially when the women concerned include others beside white, affluent feminists) would bear such a striking resemblance to the "good old God" of Christendom.'[11]

In her desire to take seriously the viewpoints of those who have normally been excluded from theological thinking, Jantzen's concerns are similar to mine in this book. Her emphasis on the diversity that such attention would reveal is echoed in the image of a choral theology of the Church that underlies this work. However, I am not sure if the women I have included in this study would form part of Jantzen's 'trustworthy community', which is made up of all those whose outlook is formed by the struggle for justice and who are willing to be open to the scrutiny of others who are struggling for justice in different areas of life.

It is clearer to see in Jantzen's writing how she has been informed by the thought of Irigaray, and the feminist community of philosophers and theologians in general, than it is to see the influence of any community outside the university world. However, she obviously intends her divine horizon to help all women to flourish – those of St Anthony's estate just as much as those of any university theology department. She does, of course, start from the assumption that traditional Christianity does not offer any women a spiritual environment that adequately fosters their health and growth. In the section that follows, this assumption will be questioned by looking at the image of God within the spiritual lives of the Northern working-class Christian women who are at the heart of this research.

All of the four churches in this study are traditional in their teaching about God. The language they use for God is exclusively male and, indeed, inclusive language for the worshippers is only slowly gaining acceptance. This, as is often the case, does not worry any of the women I interviewed. It is the way they are used to worshipping and, as will be seen later, the thought of using anything other than male language for God is incomprehensible to the vast majority of them. They are happy to sing hymns and join in liturgy in which they speak of themselves as 'men' and feel no conscious alienation in this use.

In three of the churches, the leadership is male – inescapably so as things stand at the moment. The Roman Catholic Church, of course, does not allow women to be ordained and, while the possibility does exist in the Church of England, both St Aidan's and St Mark's have rejected the idea of having a woman priest to serve with them. The exception is Green Memorial Methodist Church, which, in Patricia, has its second female minister.[12] Although many of the Catholic (Roman and Anglican) women were happy to consider the possibility of having a woman priest, despite the official position of both churches, the model that they had grown up with was exclusively male. The women interviewed did not speak of this as necessary because only a male priest could image Christ, but as a dictat that came down from above (St Justin's) or as part of their tradition (St Aidan's). The members of St Mark's were less willing to consider change in this area, insisting on the biblical idea of male headship as having continuing validity for today.

The iconography of the four churches differs considerably. In St Justin's and St Aidan's, there is an abundance of statues and both of these churches have prominent images of Christ: a copy of the Turin Shroud head in St Justin's and a figure of Christ the King on the rood screen at St Aidan's. The other two churches offer little in the way of religious iconography and none of the four churches has any visual image of God. There are plentiful images of Mary in both the Roman Catholic and Anglo-Catholic churches, which are popular sites for the lighting of candles.

So, it is in the language – rather than in the visual imagery – that the masculinity of God is enshrined. Only the Vicar of

St Aidan's will consciously try to avoid using the masculine pronoun for God, but even he would find it difficult to speak of God as
'she' when preaching to his congregation. In other words, all four
congregations are squarely in the traditional Christian mainstream
in which God is spoken of solely in masculine language, although
the teaching that God is beyond gender is present somewhere in the
background.

I was more surprised than I perhaps should have been by the
answers to my interview questions about what, if any, image of
God the interviewee had in her mind or what she would draw if
she had to produce a picture of God. In my own experience as an
Anglican priest, I know well enough the shocked reaction that
referring to God as 'she' in a sermon is likely to evoke. It was only,
therefore, my absorption in the mental world of feminist theology
that made my respondents' pictures of God as a male patriarch
come as something of a shock. In this section we will look at some
of these images in more detail, as well as the minority of others
that did not fit this standard pattern, before going on to see whether
or not these images do in fact offer any potential for spiritual
flourishing in these women's lives and an enrichment of the
theological understanding of the wider Church.

The predominating answers to the question, 'If you had to draw
a picture of God, what would you draw?', were images of a male
God, seemingly lifted straight from generations of Christian art.
A typical example is: 'A man with a beard and that robe he has
on, but a lovely face' (Tracy, from St Vincent's, in her forties).

The impression is often of a slightly older Jesus, bearded, with
long hair, robed, but above rather than below the age of 40. This
undoubtedly partly results from the sacred images that the women
have in their own homes or see in the churches, in which it is
Jesus who is most frequently represented. In a couple of cases,
direct reference was made to the respondent's own statues and
pictures (of the Sacred Heart, Jesus clothed in a rainbow) as the
source of the image. These were usually images that the women
had lived with for a long time, but not always. Helen, a long-time

member of St Aidan's, had been greatly influenced by the statue of Christ that briefly occupied the empty plinth in Trafalgar Square:

I'll tell you the one I, what I, now, it's – we talked about this in the Lent group. You know, what they've put on the statue in the square – you know, – there's the man, and it's just a man – that's what I would put. Mind, no beard, because it's a bare-faced man, isn't it, in London. That to me, now, I would put.

Only one of the interviewees, when asked about their picture of God, responded by asking whether the question referred to God the Father or God the Son. The others instinctively answered the question as if it was referring specifically to the first member of the Trinity or to a monist Godhead.

A number of the women talked about the expression on the face of this male figure:

Just somebody with a lovely smiling face, you know. Just like a kind-looking person because of, we know what he is, you know. I think I would just imagine that, you know. (Liz, from St Aidan's)

There was a general emphasis on the figure of God being one that was filled with love – often described as fatherly love – and care. The only interviewee who talked of an image of God that contained judgement as well as care came from the evangelical tradition. Her picture was of a father who 'loves and he cares and he disciplines'.[13] There were other images that also spoke to the emotional space that God occupies in these women's lives, but by using less anthropomorphic images. Ruth, a Methodist teacher, talked of God as:

A big armchair that just encircles you and is, sort of, kind of, peace, safeness . . . and that's how I see God. He's a comfortable armchair that you can go to and it doesn't matter what's gone wrong or what's about to come, it's there, it's always the same. And it gives you comfort.

There was also evidence of how the image of God could change over time. One woman spoke with amusement of her childhood picture of God as being someone dressed in white who carefully screwed the heads on to babies. Rose from St Aidan's talked of the move away from the traditional picture of the old white male to another traditional Christian symbol:

> Well, I think my version of God when I was little was an old man with a big beard. Um, I don't know, I just don't – the only picture, the only thing now is that [holding up a palm-sized plain wooden cross] . . . I've always thought of the cross. Now, you know, since I've really believed. Because you, you know, you can't sort of vision God, anything like that, but I just look at the cross.

There was just one woman who saw God revealed in a female image. This was Enid from St Justin's – a woman in her early seventies whose life was full of the children she had brought up and who still circulate around her. She did first mention biblical images of God – speaking of him 'walking the streets in sackcloth and ashes' – but then she moved on to the emotional side of the image, seeing God as 'somebody who wants to put his arms round you.' This feeling image then led her on to remember her mother-in-law and find in her the best image she knew of God:

> When we had the kids and they were all between five and eight years – so you can imagine when we went to our families I used to think they don't want us here with this tribe, you know – but Peter's mother was always at the door with her arms open. And I used to think 'Ee, you're just like God – always welcoming people' and I adored her for it because she was a wonderful mother-in-law.

Enid never failed to talk of God as 'he' during her interview, but she also obviously felt no discontinuity in seeing God in the person of her mother-in-law. She did not feel distanced from God by her use of male pronouns and had the freedom to picture God in a non-traditional way.

All these women would claim that their male images of God were positive rather than oppressive, though this is not the language that they would naturally use. In the interviews, I asked them if they felt any distance between themselves and God because their images of God were male. A typical answer is that given by Ruth, a member of Green Memorial Methodist Church:

ELLEN: And you've never felt that you would be less in the image of God than a man?

RUTH: Oh heavens no! No! (Laughs)

The idea was dismissed in every case, with no need felt for introspection or careful thought. I began to feel foolish for asking the question when it was met with such ready negation and almost incomprehension. The reasons for not perceiving a barrier, when they were able to be articulated, clustered around two concepts: the first, that there was no real division between the genders in any case, and the second, that their experiential closeness precluded the existence of any barriers. Their God was close and their God was male and there was no need for this to change.

The images that came up in the interviews both reflect and reveal the role that these women expect God to play in their spiritual and material lives. God is the protector, the loving Father who ensures that they come to no ultimate harm, despite the pains and problems of their everyday lives. He is the one who holds their hands when there is no one else to do so. He is the one who has power and control over events and has their best interests at heart. He is the benefactor who has given them everything that they value in their lives – especially, he is the one who has given them their families – and the one who will give them their ultimate reward after death. He may also be the judge, but this judging role is generally confined to other people – the criminal and wicked or those of other beliefs.

In other words, God is the one with power over their lives, power that they do not believe they have themselves. This is not necessarily the power to change their circumstances, but to give them the strength and comfort they need to survive their circumstances. In the stories of personal tragedy that these women had to tell – of losing a child to death or the drug culture, mothering their younger brothers and sisters after the early death of their mother, for example – it was God and their faith that they believed had provided them with the strength to continue living. A typical prayer is that described by Ivy: 'I just ask the Lord, I pray that he'll help us get through another day.'

There were also expressions of anger that God could have let these things happen to them. This is the old ethical dilemma of a good and omnipotent God allowing bad things to happen in his world. Enid, after the premature death of a disabled baby, remembers feeling very angry towards God. When I asked her if, as a consequence of this experience, she had felt hatred towards God, she replied, 'I did at the time. Oh I did. I hated him for doing that to me.'[14] God has to take responsibility for the bad as well as the good in life. Again, it is God, rather than the women, who has power and control.

This powerful God, as has already been seen, is male in most of these women's spiritual imaginations. This seems inevitable when their church background is considered. They have not only been taught to speak of God in exclusively male language and picture God in exclusively male iconography, but have also seen religious leadership as exclusively male, though this has recently changed for the Methodists. What is more interesting is to see how these images are used by the women and how they have made them their own. In the next section, we will look particularly at how a male God allows for passionate engagement and see that the romantic mysticism of medieval women religious is still alive and well within the contemporary Church.

In order to look at the question of whether or not a male God can allow women to flourish spiritually, it is helpful to focus on one particular example, in which the person of Jesus is the subject of the woman's spiritual experience. Marie, who is in her sixties, converted to Roman Catholicism about 30 years ago and has also been very involved with a local ecumenical charismatic group. Her life has not been without tragedy. She lost her only son in a traffic accident a few years before the interview and works hard to keep in touch with her grandchildren, who live in London. Her husband, a cradle Roman Catholic, shares her faith, but not seemingly with the same passion.

Marie's imaginary picture of God immediately focused on Jesus:

> The way I kind of like see him, he's still got the long hair – similar to that [pointing to a picture of Jesus in a long white robe surrounded by a rainbow], that's how I always see him.

Her relationship with this God is intimate and complicated, with a romantic intensity that has strong resonances with the medieval Rhineland mystics. This passage deserves quoting at length as it encapsulates the nature of the relationship:

> I went out and bought him a record, 'cos I went through this stage, you know, when he was miles away, you know: I felt as if he wasn't answering my prayers or anything. So I went out and I went and got this record and it was that one 'Why Do You Have to Be a Heartbreaker'? And I went, 'Are you listening Lord? I'm playing this record for you.' And I played it in the room you know all the time. 'Are you listening now?', you know, 'Are you listening now?' And then I got the words from him you know, they kind of like – he was so close and he was killing himself laughing. And he says to us, he says, 'Eh well, Marie, to think that you went out and got that record just for me, I'm so pleased that you even thought of it.' He was so happy 'cos I'd gone out and got that record for him to show that I really missed him, you know. And I thought, 'Ee, he loves me that much he wants me to do things like that', you know, to show

that, um, you know, that we're really thinking of him and that. It does hurt, things like that, when he's not around, you know. He was so happy that day when I was playing it to him, you know, and, um, and then he was all right for a while after that. (Laughs)

For Marie, God is the one who responds to her love, the one whose companionship she values above all others and the one who ultimately makes life worth living. Her realisation of the value of her own self is intimately linked with her perception of God's love for her and her ability to provoke a response from this ultimate lover. The knowledge of God's presence is Marie's source of strength and comfort, which allows her to survive the tragedies and daily frustrations of her life: 'I could carry on through this life with him, but I couldn't carry on without him.'

Marie's perspective closely mirrors that of the Pentecostal women in R. Marie Griffith's study, *God's Daughters: Evangelical Women and the Power of Submission*.[15] Indeed she, like one of the Pentecostal women, received a gift of red roses that she interpreted as being a present directly from Jesus. Marie said that she had a verse about roses pop into her head when she was praying and, half an hour later, a man from across the street brought her a bunch of them:

He comes in the shop and he says, 'Oh, I picked these out of my garden for you today'. He says, 'Here's a little present for you'. Well I knew, ee, I stood there and looked at him and I was flabbergasted, 'cos I knew the Lord had sent the roses for us through somebody else for me, you know.

In exactly the same way, a recent widow interviewed by Griffith knew that the red roses given her by friends really came from Jesus:

I hold them in my arms and smell their sweetness. As I lift my face from them, I know without any hesitation or doubt that despite the card, these roses have come from Jesus. He knew I needed such a gift at this precious moment: the type of gift that a man sends a woman, a husband gives his wife. It is just one more way of saying that Jesus has become my husband, one more way He is saying 'I love you'.[16]

Griffith sees great similarities between the women's view of God/ Jesus and the characteristics of fictional romantic heroes, as analysed by Janice Radway in her influential work *Reading the Romance: Women, Patriarchy and Popular Literature*.[17] God, like these heroes, is strong and masculine, yet loving and tender: a perfect combination for the perfect husband.

In order to decide whether or not such an identification is helpful or detrimental, it is useful to refer to some of the more recent feminist work on romance, especially Wendy Langford's *Revolutions of the Heart*[18] and *Romance Revisited*, edited by Lynne Pearce and Jackie Stacey.[19] In the latter book, Rosalynn Voaden makes an interesting comparison between medieval mysticism and modern romance,[20] drawing out some of the similarities of both language and plot. She points out how courtship now, and visions then, allow women to step out of the sidelines and take a position centre stage. However, now, as then, it is only the relationship to the male (lover or God) that makes this transition possible. However, the medieval mystic had an advantage in that her adventure did not come to an end at marriage, but could be endlessly repeated: 'Whereas modern romance, and the book, end with marriage, for the medieval holy woman the last chapter could be replayed over and over again.'[21] Both mystics and romantic heroines receive their identity and self-worth as a result of being picked by the male figure and 'it is still the male who occupies centre stage'.[22]

A romantic relationship with God can be seen to fill many of the same needs for the women interviewed as for the medieval mystics. They have a perfect male figure whose love for them is beyond question and conveys a great sense of self-worth. They do not receive the public acclaim, or notoriety, that went with mystical visions in the Middle Ages, but they do gain immeasurably in their own valuation from this affirmative relationship. Wendy Langford's work supplies additional reasons for the importance of this romantic element to their religion. She sees romantic relationships between men and women as essentially destructive, in that they inevitably fail to fulfil their initial promise to meet the psychological needs of each partner.[23] Like religion, romance offers a breakthrough moment in which normal constraints are set aside: 'Hannah's comparison of romantic love with a religious experience was echoed in other accounts, which employed "spiritual" language to describe the feeling of being something higher or better.'[24] However, the romantic relationship is not strong enough to stop these constraints returning once the threshold moment has passed. This leaves men and women constantly seeking the partner with whom the breakthrough moment will miraculously last and so allow their deepest psychological desires to be met:

> Why do we remain so loyal to the romantic ideal? Ultimately, the strength of our deluded attachments depends upon the *spiritual* significance that love has in our lives . . . Despite everything we believe in love. We have faith in love. We have a blind faith in love.[25]

It may be that one source of strength that the interviewees gain from their male images of God is this very fulfilment of the need for a romantic love figure. In Jesus, they have the perfect romantic partner whose interest never wanes and whose love is never defensively withdrawn.[26] The relationship is able to offer them psychological comfort without any accompanying psychological demand that they perform the role of perfect lover in return. Langford's book ends with the question, 'If we loosen our attachments and begin to see love for what it is, we cannot but face a crisis of faith for if not love, what then would we place our hearts upon?'[27] The religious images of these women may provide an answer. Their hearts, while also being full of family and friends, are also set on a heavenly lover. Having found this love, they are then free to put their energy into living rather than the endless round of romantic search and disappointment. On the negative side, they are still left, as Voaden pointed out, with a male figure at the centre of the universe and not encouraged to see fulfilment within their own image.

It is interesting to see how, in listening to the stories of these working-class women from the North East of England, we also hear echoes of voices from further afield. In the United States, black women theologians also point to the central role of Jesus in the theology and spirituality of the black communities. This can be seen in the work of two prominent womanist theologians, Jacquelyn Grant[28] and Delores Williams, who point to the importance of the figure of Jesus for the spirituality of black women and, as a result, are reluctant to endorse feminist theologies that lose the historical individual in a universal Christ, or Christa.[29] Jesus, rather than being the perfect lover, is more typically the fellow sufferer who understands the pain that black women endured, both during the time of slavery and in the racist era that has succeeded it. He is a key figure in black women's ability to survive – even to thrive – in the midst of adversity and prejudice: 'And the story of black Christian women's fortitude cannot be accurately told without Jesus, whom these women have historically regarded as their helpmate on their journey.'[30] God the Father plays a less central role in black American women's theology, where it is more often the Spirit who is the focus of worship, says Susan Thistlethwaite.[31] She is also at pains to point out that the black women's tradition includes images of God as mother alongside those of God as father. Thus, God is 'father to the fatherless, mother to the motherless', carrying the complete parental role rather than only the male aspect.

There is not space in this book to investigate the question of the parallels between race prejudice in the United States and class prejudice in Britain and the possible resonances in the subsequent experiences of women in these two categories. However, there are striking similarities in the role that religion seems to play in their lives. Delores Williams makes innovative use of the story of Hagar to explore the suggestion that womanist theology centres on survival and the quality of life rather than on liberation from the current social order.[32] In her article in Ursula King's *Feminist Theology from the Third World: A Reader*,[33] Williams identifies these as key issues highlighted by Alice Walker, who first introduced the concept of womanist writing:

> Walker simultaneously affirms black women's historic connection with men through love and through a shared struggle for survival and for productive quality of life (i.e. 'wholeness'). This suggests that two of the principle concerns of womanist theology should be survival and community building and maintenance.[34]

These same priorities come through in the voices of the white women of the East End of Newcastle. They are not excited by the prospect of revolutionising their social milieu, but they are motivated by a need to make the best of the circumstances in which they find themselves and to do so while keeping their ties with family and community intact. Their spiritual experiences affirm them in their present place and offer them a form of male affirmation that they may not find elsewhere.

The male figures of God provide the women with the most affirming male presence in their lives. This God does not devalue them because of their gender – in fact, many of them described him as being gender blind: 'I don't think God sees wer as men and women. I think he sees wer as his family, his children, you know. You know I can't see any difference at all.'[35]

Their value in God's eyes is diminished neither by the fact that they are women, nor that they are working class and struggling financially. They see themselves as having just as close contact with divine love and favour as those who hold the power in society, although none of those interviewed expressed the liberation theology idea of God having a preferential option for the poor and dispossessed. Their relationship with God offers them an unqualified affirmation that is lacking from their social relationships as a whole. It is an area of life in which they can feel that they have succeeded as they may not possess social power, but they do have a connection to the source of all power, who confirms them in their own self-worth.

The quotation from Marie showed that this relationship with divine power may contain a heterosexual romantic aspect. The love between the women and God is not a generalised religious benevolence, but a more passionate encounter of the self with the ultimate person. The male gender of this ultimate person arises both from Church teaching and the social hierachy, in which men still hold power and are in positions of control. God provides the ultimate authority that vindicates these women's lives and overrules any divisions, and denigrations, arising from class and gender. This God also provides the perfect male companionship, combining the approving gaze of the loving father with that of the faithful lover. Through this connection to a loving and powerful male, the women feel able to cope with life and survive their marginalised position. They are both comforted and enabled to continue facing life with courage:

> I mean, me divorce and all different things like that and he's just pulled me through it. Now I do honestly truly believe it was him that's brought us through, 'cos I never, I never had the strength to do it myself. (Rose, from St Aidan's)

The women are aware of what their needs are and at the moment these needs are best met by a strong male image of God.

Having identified much that is valuable about these images of God, it is also necessary to reflect on how, from a contemporary theological viewpoint, they are flawed and incomplete. The most obvious problem is that, although these images are empowering for the women, in so far as they provide support and comfort and validation, they do not provide a symbol of empowered *women*.

Their images of strength and control are all male. When the women in the interviews were asked if they did, or could, use female imagery and language to speak of God, the result was a resounding negative. The following answers are typical:

ELLEN: Some women theologians would like us to use female language of and for God as well as male language – mother
as well as father. How would you feel about that?
MONICA: I've heard that question before, and I don't know
whether I could get used to that, I don't know ... I
fully understand the question you're saying, but I don't
feel I could somehow, you know.

ELLEN: Do you always think of God in male terms?
HELEN: Yeah. Aha. Oh yes. I'm not going to say 'Our Mother',
no, no. God the Father – that's him.
ANGELA: I can relate to him as God my Father – I can say without
any problems at all – but I couldn't – I couldn't worship
and pray or anything in a female form because it would
feel alien to me, it would feel all wrong.[36]

Female imagery and female language are not seen to have any connection with the God of their spiritual experience. Thinking in these terms would mean stepping outside the borders of the ortho-dox and, as Angela went on to say, would be 'almost blasphemy'.

Irigaray and Jantzen are both right when they point to the diffi-culty of women seeing themselves in the divine image within main-stream Christian spirituality. There is no divine image with which the women can identify as women, no divine horizon that provides them with a blueprint for their own spiritual development and flourishing. The only possible exception to the uniformity of male language and imagery for God is found in the devotion to the Virgin Mary expressed by many of the Roman and Anglo-Catholic women. The possibility that this provides an alternative divine imagery for the Church, and for the women interviewed, will be discussed next.

The Marian dimension to spirituality was limited, as is only to be expected, to those women in the study who identified themselves as Catholic and belonged to St Justin's and St Aidan's. The Methodist women and those from the evangelical parish of St Mark's made no mention of Mary, either positive or negative. Liz, one of the members of St Aidan's, also found the emphasis on Mary disturbing:

> I do think it's a bit like that – a bit 'false god' sort of thing. Well it is, yes. I think they make Mary – have Mary on a par with God – and that's not right somehow.

Disquietude with the role of Mary within the Church can be found in a considerable body of academic theological thought also, as will be seen. However, there are others, within liberation and feminist theology, who believe that Mary offers possible relief from the masculine focus of Christianity as a whole. In this section I will look at the very different roles that Mary plays in feminist spirituality and theology, laying these alongside the place and purpose that she fills in the spiritual lives of the Roman and Anglo-Catholic women of the East End.

One important aspect of the interviewing process was the opportunity it gave me to talk to the majority of the women within their own home setting. This provided an insight into the impact that their faith had on their domestic surroundings. In particular, it was interesting to see the comparative number of statues and pictures of Jesus and Mary in the homes of the Catholic interviewees. In both Roman Catholic and Anglican homes, Jesus was outnumbered two to one by Mary.[37] The images were not high art (although one woman did have a living room crammed with reproductions of old masters, which included da Vinci's *Virgin of the Rocks*), but were clearly devotional in nature. Favourite statues were of the Immaculate Heart and the Sacred Heart, while pictures focused on modern images of Mary or Jesus with European features and welcoming smiles. In some cases, the interviewees mentioned images that were kept elsewhere in the house – usually in t, bedroom, but, in one case, there was also a small shrine to Mary in the back yard.

Whenever I mentioned Mary in the interviews, she was immediately referred to as either 'the Blessed Virgin Mary' or, more usually, 'Our (Blessed) Lady', with an emphasis that tended to suggest it was unsuitable to speak of her by her name alone. This immediately suggests the reverence in which Mary is held. This was epitomised in the answer given by Vera, a member of St Justin's now in her seventies, when asked to describe God. Having described God the Father by reference to Michelangelo's *Creation of Adam* in the Sistine Chapel, she continued:

> The three persons in one God? I always think of Jesus like that [pointing to a statue of the Sacred Heart] and I like to think of him being a little baby in that stable in Bethlehem. Our Lady, well I think of her as – I'll show you the statue in the living room before you go. She just looks so young and serene.

Vera unconsciously segues straight into the description of Mary from the description of Jesus, her instinct being to see her as the third member of the Trinity. When asked directly about any image she might have of the Holy Spirit, she is aware of the minor place he plays in her spiritual life: 'The Holy Spirit? He's quite often in the form of a dove isn't he? Perhaps I should think a bit more about the Holy Spirit than I do, Ellen.' Vera is, of course, consciously aware that the Trinity is Father, Son and Holy Spirit, but this theological truth is not a true reflection of her internal spiritual Trinity. Her prayers are addressed to 'Jesus, Our Lady and St Joseph', while she sees God the Father as being in overall control.

Vera is not exceptional in this. It is hard to overemphasise the role that Mary plays in the spiritual lives of many of these women. Marie, whose romantic relationship with Jesus was discussed earlier, was, at first, almost exclusively focused on Mary:

Mary at the beginning, it was all like Mary, you
the beginning ... I mean, I was in love with this
ـ ـ ـ oved God and I loved Mary, but Jesus, poor soul, was
out of it.

It was Mary who led Marie to Jesus by telling her that she ought
to start learning more about her son. Mary also figures in the
religious experiences that the women describe. Rose from St Aidan's
told me about an experience she had in the Roman Catholic Chapel
(known as the Slipper Chapel) during the church's annual pilgrim-
age to Walsingham. She was in a wheelchair at the time and, while
she was praying, she felt herself being gently rocked back and forth
– 'just like somebody moving a baby back and forwards, like that'.
Rose agreed with a nun, to whom she told the story, that the
experience had been a blessing given to her by Our Lady. Monica
and Marie from St Justin's also talked about mystical or mysterious
experiences associated with Mary. In one story, her icon was saved
from the midst of a kitchen fire and, in another, she appeared in
a vision to lead the recipient of the vision back to the Church.

Devotion to Mary is encouraged at both St Aidan's and
St Justin's, with the weekly rosary group at the latter playing a
large part in its adherents' spiritual lives.[38] Links are strengthened
by regular pilgrimages to Walsingham and Lourdes, which provide
both cheap holidays and a heightening of spiritual intensity. The
relationship with Mary had the same depth as the relationship with
Jesus. Our Lady, like Our Lord, is the human and approachable face
of God. Although theological language was not used, the impression was given that they both incarnated God: Mary as well as
Jesus provided a human face for God. They are needed not because
God is seen as frightening and remote but because they, unlike
God, have undergone the suffering of human life and can be
counted on to understand what their followers are going through.
This is particularly true of Mary's experience of motherhood. This
resonates with the women in two ways. First, in Mary they see a
figure who mothers them and is there to answer their needs:

I mean she's always been special to us, you know. She's been my special mother – that's how I think of her. (Enid, from St Justin's)

Second, they see in her a companion of their own motherhood:

I often use the image of her by the cross, you know – watching her son suffer. And, you know, I sort of use that myself if I feel I'm suffering through the kids. (Monica, from St Justin's)

Mary as mother is both the ever-comforting figure to whom they can turn, as to their own mother, and the one who understands the pain of bringing up a family. There was no talk of Mary's virginity: it did not seem that this was in any way questioned, but it did not play a conscious part in the spiritual relationship.

One of the women interviewed, Liz, a member of St Aidan's in her forties, offered an explanation for the Catholic devotion to Mary, a devotion that she did not herself share. She spoke first of her impatience with all the 'Mary, Mary, Mary' and her feeling that prayers ought to be addressed to God alone. She went on to say that she could see why Mary might be reverenced as the mother of Jesus, but that she had never felt any particular connection with her personally: 'I've never even thought about praying to Mary – not even in pregnancy or losing babies.' Her thinking took her further when she put together her own sense of God as male with the reverencing of Mary:

But, no, I don't think I could be comfortable with him [God] as a woman – as a female. No, this must be why Mary is very highly reverenced by people – because they want the woman figure.

Although Liz professed herself satisfied with the male image of God that she holds, she could see that Mary might fill a gap for other people by providing a female image of God to complement the male.

Liz's comments would be welcomed by some feminist theologians for whom Mary offers a positive site for the female within patriarchal Christianity. This is not the case for all feminist commentators, though, as will be seen. Mary is a controversial figure within feminist theology, being identified both as the best hope for redeeming Christianity and also as one of the main tools used by a patriarchal Church to keep women firmly in their place. This section will look at both poles of the argument and see where the experience of the Catholic women of these North Eastern churches fits in to, or disrupts, this theorising.

Marina Warner in *Alone of All Her Sex*[39] is one who has found the symbolism of Mary a stumbling block on her spiritual journey. Warner sees in Mary the valorisation of an impossible ideal for women – the classic double-bind of women having to retain their virginity to be accorded moral worth, while at the same time being allowed fulfilment only through motherhood. Against the emotional appeal of Marian devotion, Warner sets her feminist reasoning: 'But though my heart rebelled, I held fast to my new intimation that in the very celebration of the perfect human woman, both humanity and women were subtly denigrated.'[40] Mary, the perpetual virgin and sentimentalised mother, also seems to offer no foothold for a feminist symbol in the view of the womanist theologian Delores Williams.[41] Williams criticises the way that Mary was held up to black women in the United States as a model of gentleness and domesticity: a role model that, if imitated, would lead to acceptance of their position rather than providing the impetus for liberating change. Her criticism of Marian devotion goes on to point out the diminution it causes to the role of Joseph and she later suggests that the ability to relate to Mary, or otherwise, may be class-related.

A more positive assessment of the potential of the figure of Mary is found in the writing of Mary Daly, although she also is very critical of the way that Mary has been presented by the patriarchal

Church. She, along with Warner, sees Mary's virgin motherhood as having a punitive function in relation to ordinary women, but also sees the possibility of Mary taking on a new symbolic role: 'Symbolically speaking, it is the Virgin who must free and "save" the Son'.[42] Mary is, for Daly, the only possible source of spiritual nourishment in Christianity for women, and she quotes with approval Elizabeth Gould Davis' declaration that, 'the only reality in Christianity is Mary, the Female Principle, the ancient goddess reborn.'[43] However, Daly's interest in Mary has waned along with her interest in Christianity as a whole and her radical rereading of her is far beyond the shores of orthodox Christianity.

Mary has also been rediscovered by other feminist writers who would want to stay closer to the teachings of the Church. Of particular note are the Latin American theologians Ivone Gebara and Maria Clara Bingemer, whose important book *Mary: Mother of God, Mother of the Poor*[44] sums up a strong current in liberation theology. The title almost says it all: Mary is rediscovered as the representative of all oppressed and marginalised people, who are seen to share in Mary's honour and exaltation. Gebara and Bingemer are able to see in Mary a radically free human being who plays an active role in the redemption of the world.

They even put value on her virginity – a traditional sticking point for feminist theologians, who see in the doctrine of the virgin birth a denial of the worth of female sexuality. On the contrary, Gebara and Bingemer see in Mary's virginity a symbol of her radical freedom from all patriarchal ties, allowing her the liberty to say 'yes' to God in her own right, a view taken up by Chung Hyun Kyung: 'Asian women are beginning to view the virginity of Mary, not as a *biological* reality, but as a *relational* reality.'[45]

The Virgin Mary is the model of the poor woman who is yet able to speak as she is in some measure free from patriarchal control, and what she speaks is the message of justice and liberation of the Magnificat. Rosemary Radford Ruether also sees in Mary a figure of liberation, she is the 'new thing' that God is bringing into being as eschatological freedom breaks down all barriers constructed by patriarchy and all hierarchy. This, rather than the ideal of passive, receptive femininity, is, for Ruether, the true message of Mariology.[46]

One of the most interesting recent books on Mariology is Tina Beattie's *God's Mother, Eve's Advocate*, in which she attempts to stay within the context of Roman Catholic orthodoxy while reinterpreting patristic teaching about Mary in a way that opens up the priesthood to women. Beattie emphasises the traditional connection between Mary and Eve, in which Eve is redeemed through Mary, and extends this to suggest that Mary frees all women from the domination of the male. Mary, in her view, is a partner with Christ in the work of human salvation, though not a divine figure. God in Godself remains beyond gender in divine transcendence, which is 'the place of fertile encounter' between the sexes, but God's immanence is known both in man and woman, in Christ and in Mary.

It is here that it is possible to hear echoes of the women's interpretation of their spiritual experience as revealed in their interviews. When they speak of God as a transcendent being, they inevitably use the male pronoun and have male images at the forefront of their mind. This is the case even when they also make mention of their belief that God is beyond gender. They have thoroughly internalised the Church's teaching that God is Father and find the thought of using female language for God distasteful and unsettling. However, when they speak of God as immanent, as appearing to them in dreams and visions or as talking to them in prayer, they speak of both Jesus and Mary in language that makes them of equivalent importance. The immanent God comes to them as both male and female, as Son and as Mother. As Ivy said when explaining why she would not call God mother: 'I mean, to me, Mary's the one – if you want to pray to a mother, you pray to Mary.'

These Roman and Anglo-Catholic women would, I feel, have no difficulty in accepting Beattie's emphasis on Mary as companioning Jesus in the process of redemption. Their interest, however, is not in seeing her as a perpetual virgin, free from the restrictive ties of patriarchal relationships, but as the mother who has suffered through her child. Mary has not been set free from the romantic sentimentalisation that has surrounded her image in Western Christianity: the hymn regularly sung at the rosary group includes the line 'I weep at your beauty' and is unashamedly a love song. Mary is important not as a woman who has transcended patriarchal forms of relationship, but as a woman whose essence is relationality: she is Mary the mother both in relation to God and in relation to humanity. In this identity, she gives to the women who reverence her primarily comfort, both as the eternal mother who will always love and care for them and as the eternal mother who shares their experiences of motherhood, both joyful and painful. Only secondarily could she be said to offer to them an exemplar of redeemed humanity or redeemed womanhood. This is because she remains a figure in the divine rather than in the human sphere, to be reverenced rather than imitated.

It is obvious from the above that the women I interviewed felt that they gained great personal help from their relationship with a male God and, for many, a motherly Virgin Mary. God is both the perfect Father, offering protection and comfort, and, in Jesus Christ, the perfect lover/husband, offering unconditional regard and romantic constancy. God is 'he' both because 'he' is the pronoun of the powerful and those in control and, in this heterosexual context, is the source of romantic, transformative love. Being in relationship with such a God offers personal affirmation and the satisfaction of needs for recognition and validation that are not met elsewhere. Leavening this male influence, for the Catholic women at least, is the presence of the Virgin Mary, giving them the reassurance that, despite the loss of their own mother, they still have a motherly, nurturing presence in their lives. Intellectually, they do not see her as another form of God, but their spiritual experience is of a divine love that is known in the form of 'Our Lady' as well as in the form of 'Our Lord'.

These images of God do not sit comfortably with feminist sensibilities, my own included. The whole concept of romantic love is deeply suspicious to many feminist academics, although directing these feelings to a transcendent God seems, perhaps surprisingly, to offer a less debilitating outlet for them than to attach them to one particular man. More worryingly, these images seem to offer no 'divine horizon' that Jantzen and Irigaray would see as crucial for women to flourish spiritually. The divine is male and the only female characteristic that reaches close, though still falls short of divinity, is motherhood. The male images of God remain resolutely other to the women's own identities and do not appear to offer any routes for approaching female divinisation. While the Virgin seems emotionally to offer a female incarnation of divine love, she still remains outside the Godhead and so does not offer a satisfactory model of the female divine.

However, divinisation is not these women's primary need – if we allow them the right to assess their own needs, rather than having them defined from outside. They need and value an image of God that provides them with support and encouragement here and now rather than one that would enable growth in the future. It is easy for middle-class, affluent, socially successful academics to say that all these needs could be met by a female image of God – a strong, womanly presence that provides both affirmation in the present and a model of becoming for the future. However, introducing such an image should not be seen as a simple corrective action, to be undertaken in the spirit of feminist evangelism, as some feminist theologians seem to suggest. This would only serve to both undermine the self-validation that these women currently gain from their relationships with their Father/Lover God and trivialise their understanding of their own spiritual experiences. The Church would also lose a distinctive and passionate seam of spirituality that reaches back to medieval times and continues to enrich women's lives today.

Instead, it is essential for the academy and the wider Church to recognise the value that these women receive from their images of God, however limited they may seem to be from some standpoints. It might then be possible to look at ways that these images might be supplemented, rather than supplanted, by female imagery of the divine. In many ways, this is a harder path to tread than advocating the replacement of male with female imagery as it involves stepping outside the imagery with which we are, or I am, comfortable in order to recognise that which is of value to the other. It is these voices that must be included within Jantzen's 'trustworthy community' if the theology of the Church is to escape the trap of being yet another theology of, and for, the elite.

So the wider Church, and the academy, needs to hear the worth within the traditional images of God that these working-class women use in their private devotion and as part of their communal worship. This is not to say that insights from academic theology – including feminist theology – have nothing to offer within this working-class context. However, it is the listening that should come first, and only then the process of seeing how other spiritual insights and experience might add to, rather than take away from, the existing spirituality. There is a necessary humility involved in this: the acceptance that our own spirituality is limited by our particular experiences and understandings, the willingness to stand to one side and allow the other to share the space of the Church, the belief that we may still have something to learn.

Part of this process also involves looking at the context – not merely the content – of our, and their, spirituality. In other words, it may only be by changing some of the social conditions under which these women live their lives that the insights, for example, of feminist theology can have a real impact on them. It is more than an ethical imperative that issues of justice and spirituality should be linked, it is a practical necessity for spiritual change of any depth. In order for female images of the divine to resonate, there has to be the validation of women in this social grouping. The image must bear some likeness to reality if it is to convince spiritually.

The apophatic tradition within Christianity constantly reminds us that all of our language and imagery of God is partial and inadequate. God is always far more than we can describe in words or even imagine in the silence of our hearts and minds. This acknowledgement allows a certain spaciousness within the understanding of the Church – there is room for other Christians' inadequate images as well as for our own. This insight is at the heart of a choral theology, in which the one tune of praise to God is sung together but by different voices using their own language of the heart.

Notes

1 The academy in this context is shorthand for professional theologians and the whole world of academia.
2 This term refers to feminist writers who began their theology within a Christian framework, but have since moved away from Christianity. The American writers Mary Daly and Carol Christ, along with British writer Daphne Hampson, are examples of this movement.
3 Luke 15.3–10.
4 Genesis 1.27 (NRSV).
5 A thealogian is a person who studies the Goddess as opposed to a theologian who studies God.
6 Quoted by Grace Jantzen in *Becoming Divine: Towards a Feminist Philosophy of Religion*, Manchester: Manchester University Press, 1998, p. 15, from Luce Irigaray's *Sexes and Genealogies*, Gillian C. Gill (translator), originally published by Columbia University Press in 1987.
7 'So when are we to become women?' in Luce Irigaray, *Je, Tu, Nous: Toward a Culture of Difference*, Alison Martin (translator), New York: Routledge, 1993, p. 138.
8 *Becoming Divine* p. 89, emphasis as in the original.
9 *Becoming Divine*, p. 161.
10 *Becoming Divine*, p. 274, emphasis as in the original.
11 *Becoming Divine*, p. 108.
12 However, this should not lead one to imagine that issues of female authority are completely resolved within the local Methodist circuit. The female superintendent of the circuit resigned in 2001 because she found the pressures brought on her as a woman leader were too great to cope with.

13 Jane, a member of St Mark's in her late forties.

14 Enid, a member of St Justin's, was able to begin forgiving God after seeing a television programme showing a family torn apart by the mother's obsessive care for her disabled child. She felt that this programme had been sent to her by God.

15 Berkeley: University of California Press, 1997.

16 *God's Daughters*, p. 130.

17 Chapel Hill: University of North Carolina Press, 1984.

18 *Revolutions of the Heart: Gender, Power and the Delusions of Love*, London: Routledge, 1999.

19 London: Lawrence & Wishart, 1995.

20 'The language of love: medieval erotic vision and modern romance fiction', pp. 78–88.

21 *Romance Revisited*, p. 80.

22 *Romance Revisited*, p. 87.

23 In Langford's view, each partner is seeking the perfect parenting relationship with the parent of the opposite sex that they failed to have as children. The relationship dynamics mirror those of Hegel's master–slave dyad, with the woman, of course, in the position of the slave.

24 *Revolutions of the Heart*, p. 35.

25 *Revolutions of the Heart*, concluding paragraph, p. 153, emphasis as in the original.

26 This 'romantic Jesus' became a familiar figure from the late nineteenth century onwards, with such works as Ernst Renan's *Life of Christ*.

27 *Revolutions of the Heart*, p. 153.

28 See particularly Grant's *White Women's Christ and Black Women's Jesus: Feminist Christology and Womanist Response*, Atlanta: Scholars, 1989.

29 'Christa' is the term used when Christ is pictured in female form.

30 Delores S. Williams, *Sisters in the Wilderness: The Challenge of Womanist God-Talk*, New York: Orbis, 1996, p. 202.

31 See the chapter 'God the Father, God the Mother, and the Goddess' in Susan Thistlethwaite, *Sex, Race and God: Christian Feminism in Black and White*, New York: Crossroad, 1989.

32 See *Sisters in the Wilderness*, as above.

33 London: SPCK, 1994.

34 'Womanist theology: black women's voices', in Ursula King (ed.)

Feminist Theology from the Third World: A Reader, London: SPCK and Orbis, 1994, pp. 80–1.

35 Enid, from St Justin's. The exceptions to this rule were the evangelical women from St Mark's, who did feel that the sexes were created to fill different roles, though they still did not see this impacting profoundly on their relationship with God – it had more to do with their relationships with one another.

36 Monica is a member of St Justin's in her early forties, Helen is a member of St Aidan's in her late sixties and Angela is a member of St Mark's in her sixties.

37 The actual numbers were quite small. There were four statues of Mary and two of Jesus in Roman Catholic homes, and two of Mary and one of Jesus in Anglican homes.

38 This group was described in Chapter 2.

39 London: Picador, 1990 (1985).

40 From the Introduction to *Alone of All Her Sex*, quoted by Tina Beattie, *God's Mother, Eve's Advocate: A Gynocentric Refiguration of Marian Symbolism in Engagement with Luce Irigaray*, Bristol: University of Bristol, 1999, p. 110.

41 See *Sisters in the Wilderness*, Chapter 7.

42 *Beyond God the Father*, Boston: Beacon, 1973, p. 96.

43 Quoted on p. 92 of *Beyond God the Father*, from *The First Sex*, New York: G. P. Putnam's Sons, 1971, p. 246.

44 Phillip Berryman (translator), Tunbridge Wells: Burns & Oates, 1989.

45 *Struggle to be the Sun Again: Introducing Asian Women's Theology*, New York: Orbis, 1990, p. 77, emphasis as in the original. It is not, of course, only feminist liberation theologians who are interested in reassessing the role of Mary. For one of the more radical writings on Mariology, see Leonardo Boff's *The Maternal Face of God* (R. B. Barr and J. W. Diercksmeier (translators), Collins, 1987), in which he links Mary hypostatically with the third person of the Trinity, which would have delighted Jung.

46 See *New Woman, New Earth: Sexist Ideologies and Human Liberation*, 2nd edition, Boston: Beacon, 1995, Chapter 2.

4

'CHERISH HER'

One of the strongest threads running through contemporary spirituality is an emphasis on relationships – relationships between individuals, but also relationships between humanity and the rest of creation. This is particularly, but not only, true of feminist spirituality. As the British theologian Mary Grey says, 'The metaphor of connectedness has become central for the women's movement and for Christian feminist spirituality'.[1] This chapter will begin by looking at two examples of this contemporary spirituality and some of the psychological theorising that accompanies it. Alongside this will be set the relationships and spirituality of the women I interviewed, focusing particularly on motherhood as this is the relationship that constantly came to the fore as they spoke. The place of the natural world – the 'web of life' of ecological and feminist theologies – will also be considered, remembering that the immediate landscape of the St Anthony's estate is not one of readily apparent natural beauty.

Mary Bednarowski, in her survey of the religious thought of American women between 1985 and 1997, identifies five pervasive themes:

- ambivalence to established religious communities;
- the immanence of the sacred;
- the revelatory power of ordinary life;
- the primacy of physical and spiritual healing;
- a relational view of ultimate reality.[2]

Bednarowski disagrees with the American philosopher Nancy Frankenberry's assertion that this last concept, relationality, is in such common use as to be in danger of being emptied of all meaning. Instead, Bednarowski claims that:

> If one looks at how the concept of 'relationship' has fostered new understandings of the sacred and ultimate reality, of human nature and agency, and the workings of the world, then the term no longer appears over-used and under-defined, but dense and complicated with insights and meanings from many traditions.[3]

Relationship is the beating heart of American women's religious imagination, giving life to the full spectrum of religious traditions.

In Christian feminist spirituality, relationship is the defining feature both of what it means to be human and of the nature of the divine. Judith Plaskow and Carol Christ emphasise this understanding of the spiritual self in their introduction to the third part of *Weaving the Visions* (Harper & Row, 1989), tellingly entitled 'Self in Relation':

> The authors of the essays in this section agree that the self is essentially relational, inseparable from the limiting and enriching contexts of body, feeling, relationship, community, history and the web of life.[4]

Within this section, relationality is seen as an essential part of feminist ethics and divine reality, with an emphasis on the doctrine of the Trinity because this makes relationship an integral part of God's being.[5] It seems to be true that wherever you look in American feminist Christian theology, the notion of relationship will be somewhere present. This is not just true for American writings. Relationship is at the heart of the theology of Mary Grey, who, as mentioned, is a British feminist theologian. It is to her work that we will now turn.

In some ways, my theological dream mirrors Mary Grey's. We both envisage a theology that is produced by the whole Church rather than an academic elite alone: 'The hope is that *Relational* Theology will inspire a different sort of praxis and that theologising will once more be restored as the activity of the whole community-in-relationship.'[6] 'Community-in-relationship' is the central building block of Grey's thinking. It leads away from a view of redemption being a concern for the individual towards redemption as a communal aim. Within the Church, theology and action should go hand in hand, working together for the well-being of the whole human community – indeed the whole community of living beings.

The theological foundation for Grey's emphasis on relationship is found both in her understanding of the nature of God and the nature of human beings – these two ideas being so interwoven as to make it hard to decide which has priority in her thought. The title of the second chapter of her book, *Prophecy and Mysticism*, sums this up: 'In the beginning is the relation'. Grey says in this chapter that the basic structure of the human person is relational as is the structure of God's very self. In this can be seen a continuation of her line of thinking from her earlier book, *The Wisdom of Fools*: 'A metaphysic of connection sees the doctrine of God as Trinity, not in anthropomorphic terms as three males ... but as an attempt to image a God in movement, in process, a God whose whole being is to be in relation, to be relationality's core.'[7] God and humanity are both characterised by their intrinsic relationality rather than by their intrinsic individuality. So, to sum up Mary Grey's thought: God is known in relationship and as relationship and all genuine spirituality is, by definition, relational.

The foundation for this focus on relationship in Mary Grey's theology is her use and interpretation of women's experience. She feels that it is women who have had the honour, and the burden, of keeping humanity's relational values alive. Grey believes this to be the case even when the women themselves have not been aware of it: 'Whether or not historically all women have actually experienced this in their own lives at a conscious level, they have often been holding alive all humanity's yearning for deeper and more satisfying patterns of relating.'[8] It is this experience that Grey believes to have been missing from traditional Christian theology, with the result that it has failed to produce adequate ways of understanding the nature of God and humanity. Women are the ones who make connections, with other people and with the wider creation and, by so doing, they offer a new way of being Church and imagining ultimate reality. Grey is clear that this connectedness does not amount to the loss of individual identity, but the emphasis is on the kinship between all people and all the natural world, rather than on their distinctive differences. Christian living is to be expressed in 'solidarity, mutuality, interdependence and the commitment to the ongoing process of liberation'[9] rather than through individual piety and heroic acts of holiness.

Behind Grey's thinking, and that of many other feminist writers in this area, lies the influential work of the psychologists Nancy Chodorow and Carol Gilligan. Throughout Grey's work, she refers to listening to 'a different voice', partially referring to the title of Gilligan's most famous book, *In a Different Voice*,[10] and frequently mentions both Chodorow's and Gilligan's theories. Indeed, their influence has been felt throughout the field of feminist theology and spirituality, although their work has also been seriously challenged and, in some eyes, discredited.

Both Chodorow's and Gilligan's work takes place against the backdrop of the theories of Freud and Lacan. These can be explained, in an extremely simplified form, as seeing women as the half of humanity that does not fit. Women are characterised by the lack of male attributes, rather than by attributes of their own, and are thought not to have made the full transition to adulthood of their male counterparts. Our (women's) central problem is seen to be our failure to distinguish clearly enough between our own identity and that of our mothers, with a subsequent failure to become fully autonomous and stand-alone individuals.[11] Girls, and women, are defined by their continued identification

with other people while boys, and men, are defined by their understanding of their own unique individuality.

Nancy Chodorow accepts this idea that girls are more defined
by relationship than boys, but sees this as an asset rather than a
handicap: 'Specifically, I shall propose that, in any given society,
feminine personality comes to define itself in relation and connection to other people more than masculine personality does.'[12] This
is not, argues Chodorow, due to any genetic difference between
the genders, but, rather, because women, not men, in the main,
are the primary caregivers for young children. Put simply, boys
have more of a struggle to differentiate themselves from their
caregiver – because they are male and she is female – and, in the
process, build up stronger individual egos. Girls are able to continue to identify with their caregiver and so remain more open to
identification and close relationships with others. In Chodorow's
own, slightly more technical, words: 'The care and socialisation of
girls by women ensure the production of feminine personalities
founded on relation and connection, with flexible rather than rigid
ego-boundaries, and with a comparatively secure sense of gender
identity.'[13]

Chodorow's work is often used in conjunction with that of Carol
Gilligan, who considers psychological development beyond the first
years of life. Gilligan wrote in order to correct the unfairness she
saw in the work of male developmental psychologists, whose
theories of natural and healthy development seemed to rely on
male patterns and ignore possible differences between the sexes.
Her particular focus is the area of ethical judgement, in which she
challenges Kohlberg's hierarchy of moral decision making, in which
boys regularly outscore girls. Instead, Gilligan proposes a schema
in which a, typically male, ethic of rights, is compared to a, typically
female, ethic of care. This ethic of care is closely allied to women's
emphasis on relationship rather than individuality:

As we have listened for centuries to the voices of men and the
theories of development that their experience informs, so we

have come more recently to notice not only the silence of women but the difficulty of hearing what they have to say when they speak. Yet in the different voice of women lies the truth of an ethic of care, the tie between relationship and responsibility, and the origins of aggression in the failure of connection.[14]

For Gilligan, as for Chodorow, it is women who have developed relationships, while men have majored on individual, competitive achievement.

Gilligan and Chodorow have also been allied in the criticism that their theories have received. It is clear that Chodorow is not suggesting a biological basis for women's relational nature, but one that depends on the social organisation of childcare and its psychological consequences. However, her theory has still struck later writers as, if not classically essentialist, certainly too sweepingly universalistic. Gilligan is also accused of failing to take account of the differences between women and ignoring the contribution of race and class to an individual's developmental process – maximising the difference between men and women, while minimising the difference between women from different racial and class backgrounds. Her theory lends itself to an essentialism of female identity that sees it overriding any other individual characteristics and effectively silencing the voices of women who do not fit. However, despite these criticisms, both Chodorow and Gilligan have made a considerable contribution to the emphasis on relationship within feminist thought.

Indeed, it is clear that relationship is at the heart of a great deal of feminist writing on spirituality and theology, even when its psychological basis is contested. In the next section of the chapter, the theorising will be put to the test. We will see whether or not the working-class women in this research define themselves by relationships and, more widely, how their spirituality reflects their understanding or their relationships. This will help the Church in deciding how much credence should be given to the academic feminist insistence on the difference that including female experi-ence would make to Christian spirituality.

When interviewing each of the women, I began with a question that was intended to ease them into the interview and allow them to gain confidence in their ability to answer. It came out slightly differently on different occasions, but essentially it was a request for them to tell me something about themselves, something of the story of their lives so far. The question served a secondary purpose of identifying which parts of their lives the women felt were most relevant to share and what they saw as the definitive facts about themselves. This was followed up later in the interview by a direct question asking the women what they saw as being the most sig-nificant things about their lives. This provided them with a more conscious opportunity to reflect on the experiences that had most impact on their self-understanding as they selected the high or low points in the story that they had constructed from their lives.

The starting point at the beginning of the interview was, nearly always, the family into which the woman had been born. Liz, from St Aidan's, is typical of this approach:

> Well, I was born in Byker. The house that I was born in no longer exists. I'm one of seven girls. My parents have died – my mum died when I was 18, Dad died when I was 28. So we were left – I was the second eldest – so we were left to look after the subsequent five girls that were left.

It is possible that these childhood memories were edited for the interview, as they were uniformly happy, or it may be that the women of this particular group were just fortunate in their early lives.[15] Enid, from St Justin's, made a typical response: 'Well, me parents were absolutely wonderful – I couldn't fault the care I had from them.'

This contentment did not equate to financial well-being, but was felt to reside in the quality of relationships within the family unit:

I had a wonderful childhood. Not that we were well off, because we weren't. We lacked lots of things but, um, we never lacked love, we never lacked stability – in the sense of a good family.[16]

There was a realisation among the women of their good fortune in having had such a positive start in life, along with an acknowledgement that many other people had not been gifted with such satisfactory families. They saw themselves as among the lucky ones and felt that their secure background was a real blessing.

The homes in which the women grew up were, in the vast majority of cases, within a radius of ten miles of their present location, and often much closer than that. The closest was Edith, from St Aidan's: 'Here – in the room next door – not the same bed, I quite agree. But, er, yes, that's where I was born.' Many of them still had brothers and sisters close at hand, although there was also a sizeable number who had emigrated, mainly to Australia. Despite their restricted incomes, the women attempted to keep their bonds with these siblings alive and many had been over to visit on more than one occasion. Birth families, indeed, were only matched in importance by their conjugal families. The walls of most of the houses were decorated with photos of children and grandchildren and, quite often, of nieces and nephews as well. When asked about the most significant events in their lives, it was family, especially the births of children, that were most frequently cited. One notable exception to this was Tracy, from St Justin's, who, obviously equating 'significant' with 'good', replied, 'Well, marriage. I won't say children because that's been hard.' Even though disavowing children as a good and significant part of her life Tracy still talks about relationships as being at the heart of her experience.

Tracy is not alone in having problematic relationships within her close family. Although husbands and children were mostly spoken of as good things, there were exceptions, or, at least, the admittance that not everything within the family always ran smoothly:

I was introduced to a merchant seaman who I married 2 years later [age 20] and we've been married nearly 56 years. It hasn't always been great, I would be telling a lie, but we're together.[17]

Husbands were frequently spoken of in unromantic, though affectionate, terms. In some cases, they shared their wives' involvement with the Church and were sympathetic to the spiritual side of their lives. Vera, for example, met her husband when they were both singing in the choir at St Justin's and both have continued to attend the same church ever since. In slightly more cases, husbands were not involved with religion at all. Churchgoing wives usually stated that their husbands did have a faith of sorts, but that they did not feel at home in church or were not very concrete in their beliefs.[18] In only one case – that of Liz, from St Aidan's – was Christianity spoken of as a potential source of tension within the relationship:

But I've always avoided going deeper into religion because of my marriage, because Ron isn't religious. And I sometimes thought I wouldn't be able to have a good sex life if I was a Christian. I used to think years ago that Christians wouldn't do this and wouldn't do that.

Liz was able to reconcile the two parts of her life by learning that sexuality is 'a gift from God' and finding that her priorities changed as she got older. She was quite content that commitment to her religion should have come after her relationship's sexual intensity had passed its peak: 'Obviously God was wanting me to have a good time.'

Relationships with children were also causes for concern, as well as sources of the greatest fulfilment and joy. Anna, from St Aidan's, spoke of the great pain that the antagonism between two of her adult sons was causing her:

There's one thing I'd like to say to you – I've told Father Joseph, but I don't tell people at church or anything. It's awful but I feel ashamed, embarrassed. I've got three sons and, um, these two, the two older ones, they had a fall out – it must be about three year ago or so. And I know it was partly probably my fault at the time – I kept them separate because I didn't want no argument. I thought, how they say, time heals, you know . . . and, um, they don't speak still. And I pray, I pray for that. That is the only thing that sticks in my mind, why I can't have this prayer answered, you know. 'Cos I pray all the time and it never leaves my mind, never.

Anna perceived this tension as being somehow her fault, showing a far greater willingness to accept blame herself than to attribute fault to her children. She also sees the whole situation as shameful – not something like physical illness that can be shared for prayer with other people, apart from her priest. This family rift causes her more grief than her own physical disability – she suffers very badly from rheumatoid arthritis – and is the one area in which she feels that God is failing her.

There were three women interviewed who had no children: one who had remained single all her long life, one who was in her late thirties and still hoping to find a partner and one who had been physically unable to bear children with her husband. The first still had close links with her birth family, having lived with her sister until her death, and took a close interest in the families and careers of nieces and nephews. The last, Angela, from St Mark's, felt her childlessness as a burden that was eased by her relationships with other people's children: 'Didn't have any family unfortunately, but adopted hundreds of others – and sort of stand-in grandparents for the younger members of our family.'

Both these women still spoke about themselves in terms of family relationships rather than in terms of jobs, though both had worked and enjoyed doing so.[19] The younger woman still hoped for a family, although she also got a great deal of satisfaction from her spiritual life and church involvement: she is the leader of the rosary group at St Justin's.

The majority of women interviewed had worked outside the home, but in most cases the work was part-time or temporary and not seen as a career. It was usually only mentioned late on in the women's story of their lives and was seldom essential to the way they saw themselves. The exceptions to this were the four women who worked in nursing, teaching or community work. They spoke of their work in a way that made it more integral to their identity, though it was still family that had ultimate precedence. In most other cases, the work pattern fits that which Timothy Jenkins identified in his ethnography of a working-class area of Bristol: 'After marriage, women do not work for themselves but for the family.'[20]

The other relationships that the women frequently mentioned were those with neighbours and the families in their local streets. There was a fundamental divide between those in the local community whom they had known for many years and those who had recently moved on to the estate. There was a general sense of dismay that they no longer knew everyone who lived on their street:

> Um, I've always liked Byker because Byker's like, always sort of been, really friendly. Um, depend on neighbours, depend on help and never sort of feeling lonely. I always had – there was always somebody there, even not immediate family. The worst thing is now . . . I can count on one hand the number of people who I know. I mean there's people in this street – I see them come out of their front door and I think, 'Gosh, I didn't know they lived here.' I feel more closed in here and alone. Although I've got a good neighbour next door and, you know, I could bang on the wall to them and I've got a good neighbour next door on the flat, but I don't feel the same as I was when I was younger. Maybe it's because I'm getting older now, but I don't feel that same security as I did. (Rose, from St Aidan's, in her sixties)

A similar feeling of the loss of security along with familiarity was expressed when the women talked about their fear of local young people and their sense that St Anthony's had become a dump estate for troublesome families. They perceived this change in the physical care that neighbours took of their gardens and the outsides of their houses, speaking with a sense of anger and sadness about the messy and litter-strewn fronts that often bordered their own tidy plots.

The newest arrivals on the estate are asylum seekers who come from a range of different countries and cultures. Green Memorial Methodist Church plays a large part in looking after them – arranging the collection of clothing, toys and household items, as well as holding a coffee morning for them once a week. At St Aidan's, one of the few men who attend the 9.30 a.m. service is a Sri Lankan refugee, now living in one of the tower blocks near the church. These outsiders have faced some hostility and aggression in their new surroundings, with some having been attacked with air rifles as well as facing verbal taunts.

The attitude of the church women to the asylum seekers is ambivalent. They will speak of asylum seekers in general in the derogatory terms of some of the popular press, but, when faced with an individual in need, will respond with generosity and concern. This proves an interesting instance of the way in which their relationality is concrete and embodied. In the abstract, they do not immediately see any connection between themselves and impoverished people from other nations, but, when confronted with someone living among them, then the connection is made and the relationship accepted.

For these women, relationship brings responsibility as well as pleasure: as soon as a relationship is established, there are duties of care to be attended to. This is primarily true for the relationships that are founded on ties of blood, but there are also lesser obligations to those who qualify as 'neighbours'. These obligations extend from rethinking bias against asylum seekers to caring for dying relatives, as in the case of Angela, from St Mark's:

We had an old aunt who we [she and her sister] had to look after . . . I mean, it was a cantankerous old thing, actually. We looked after her to the best of our ability between us – it was difficult, but we did.

It is obvious from this quotation that familial duty had stronger imperatives than merely feelings of affection as, even when the relative was seen to be difficult or ungrateful, she still had a call on familial care. This care was primarily a female duty. It is entirely characteristic that the ageing aunt should have been looked after by her two nieces rather than by her nephews. Similarly, it is daughters who care for elderly and dying parents rather than sons, as did Rose, from St Aidan's:

When I got married I lived in the West End for a short time ... my mother wasn't very well and I used to have to come down every day ... And then of course I came back when my parents really took ill – I came back and lived over here.

It is in that 'of course I came back' that you can hear the reality of obligation within the family.

Sociological studies have shown that these networks of obligation and duty are not unique to council estates in the far North East of England. Elizabeth Roberts, in her survey of the lives of working-class women in the North West of England from 1940 to 1970,[21] identifies similar patterns of reciprocal obligation. Primary obligations are those that exist vertically across the generations – grandparent, parent, child. These are binding both up and down the chain, but there is a stronger sense of obligation from older to younger members. This view is reinforced by Marilyn Strathern, probably the most influential contemporary researcher into all forms of kinship, who finds:

the English regard children as more individualistic than parents. In the relationship between them, it seems that the parent can stand for the relationship itself, cast in terms of given ties, obligations and responsibility, while the child demonstrates the capacity to grow away from relationships, as an independent person constructing his or her own reference points,[22]

It must be said, however, that, in the data collected in my research, although it was children who did indeed stand out as having the first claim on care, parents came a very close second. Children might have grown towards independence and their own reference points, but they were still expected to sacrifice some of that independence when their parents were in positions of need.

Many of the contemporary studies of British families concentrate on those who break from the traditional model of a male and female parent with their children or, like Strathern, focus on middle-class families where there is believed to be more reflection on their own circumstances.[23] However, the women I interviewed came from traditional family structures that they mirrored in their conjugal families. They all identified themselves as heterosexual and valued long-term marital commitment. The pride of place given to family photographs in nearly every home reflects the sanctity of family within the women's belief system.

There are some sociological studies that identify similar family-centredness and look at the difference that gender plays within the family structure. This is particularly true of sociological analyses of working-class districts of Britain. Sir Raymond Firth's study of a district of South London in the 1950s and M. Young and P. Wilmott's work on Bethnal Green in the same decade are still frequently quoted. They both identify a strong family network that is primarily held together by women. In Firth's words, 'Of the households studied, knowledge of kin was usually greater among women than men. Women were pivotal to the kinship system.'[24] Wilmott and Young point out the importance of the mother–daughter link, with the mother helping the daughter with her children and then being cared for in old age by her daughter – a process facilitated by the tendency for daughters to live nearby. This pattern is echoed in C. Rosser and C. C. Harris' research on Swansea, which describes the core family unit as consisting of the parents, children and grandparents, with the wife's family being the dominant members.[25] None of these studies is very recent, reflecting the current trend to examine different rather than traditional families, but they present a striking similarity of results, which is echoed in the more recent work of Timothy Jenkins.

The largest section of Jenkins' book, *Religion in English Everyday Life: An Ethnographic Approach*,[26] centres on the working-class district of Kingswood in Bristol. Like Rosser and Harris, Jenkins finds a three-generation family at the centre of social organisation and women at the centre of the family: 'Social continuity is organised through the women: married women direct the household, they act as the accountant, and they make decisions affecting its functioning and survival.'[27] The family structure is again seen to be based on the mother–daughter link, with the men having a more peripheral role – one that allows them space to develop outside interests and means that their absence, whether temporary or permanent, does not destroy family life. It is the mother who is the focus and linchpin of the family – her home provides the venue for regular family get-togethers, which end with her death and then the focus shifts to the next generation of mothers and daughters. Jenkins summarises his findings as follows:

> In sum, local society is family-based and women-centred: the family, organised around successive generations of women and focused upon the mother, is the primary framework of continuity and response to misfortune; it is the context of mutual aid, of help, advice and services on the one hand, and of visiting, recreation and leisure on the other.[28]

Before concluding this section on sociology, it is worth looking briefly at the work of Callum Brown, who identifies some of the values that have been historically important to churchgoing women.[29] His central thesis is that religion was both privatised and feminised in the years following 1800. Women became the

105

embodiment of piety or else were socially unacceptable, having no available options but to profess 'purity and virtue, their attachment to domesticity and all the virtues located with that'.[30] They were the focus of praise for their embodiment of gentle Christian virtues of love and self-sacrifice, virtues that would serve to tame the wilder natures of their husbands and sons. Brown's conclusion is that this discourse of religious respectability now only continues to hold older women, for whom the Church has always been a central part of their self-identity. The women in my research certainly fall within this age category and it can still be useful to notice that their attitudes to relationships are shaped by this pattern of Christian responsibility. Their role as selfless givers may be part of the explanation for their place at the centre of familial relationships. Also the Church's emphasis on such virtues, historically rather than today, perhaps continues to reinforce the value they set on caring for both family and community.

The pattern of relationships in which the women provide the pivot to the whole family, is not limited to the East End of Newcastle, but seems to characterise white, working-class families more generally. It is all the more important, therefore, to understand the impact that this has on spirituality, as it will be affecting a large number of the members of the Church. This chapter will go on to consider in more detail the ways that motherhood – which is central both in sociological research and the experiences related by the interviewees – relates to their understanding of their relationship with God.

The importance of the mother–daughter relationship was unmissable in the interviews. It is exemplified by this exchange with Enid, which arose from her talking about her mother's death:

ENID: I felt very close to him [God] that night. 'Cos when you lose your mother, it's aah! Have you still got your mum?
ELLEN: I still do.
ENID: Cherish her.

She was not the only respondent to talk with particular emotion about her mother's death. Catherine, from St Mark's, identified her two worst life experiences as childlessness and the death of her mother, with her father's death being mentioned as well. Helen from St Aidan's talked of the most significant things in her life being having her children and losing her parents – 'more so my mother'. Others spoke of the continuing gap that the absence of their mother left in their life, among them Anna, from St Aidan's, now a grandmother herself:

> And, um, when I didn't feel well – I mean, Tom's marvellous, I couldn't get a better husband than him, I really couldn't – but when I used to tell my mum I felt different. I felt better when I told my mum ... I don't know, she just seemed to take everything away, you know. So I miss her when I feel down.

Although one interviewee identified her relationship with her father as being more important than that with her mother, who had been an invalid and died when she was young, the overwhelming emphasis was on their mother as the linchpin of their emotional life.

Being mothered was only matched in importance as a life experience by being a mother. It has already been seen that this is not a universally positive experience (see the quote from Tracy on p. 98), but it is of undoubted importance. This was their other primary duty of care, a duty that continued down the generations to grandchildren as well as their own children. One difference from their relationship with their own mothers was that their own children tended to live further away. Although they were usually still within Newcastle, or its northern and eastern suburbs, they were far less frequently still on the same estate. Importance was placed on having been available to the children while they were little – in Ivy, from St Justin's, words, 'I always said I'd be there all the time' – and offering continued support when it was needed, as Ruth, from St Aidan's, says:

I mean, Sophie has lived with me for seven and a half months to get that house. Sold theirs and came in here, which I've done twice for them. I says, mind, 'Never again! This is your lot!' But you know, Ellen, if she comes tomorrow and says, 'Mum can we come in?', like, I would say 'Yes'.

It was a cause of sadness to many of the women that their children failed to share their faith and did not come with them to church or attend where they now lived. It was far more common to see grandmothers and grandchildren together in church than to see mothers and their children.

The influence of grandmothers is still felt widely on the local estates. The previous incumbent of St Aidan's played a part in diffusing a potential riot in the 1990s at a time when rioting had broken out in other local areas. This was achieved by talking by name to the young men involved and threatening to let their grandmothers know how they were behaving. As in the ethnographic and sociological research cited previously, it is mothers and grandmothers who define families and who are at the centre of family discipline. This is not a culture where 'wait till your father gets home' is a common maternal threat. It is this pattern of family life that seems to have given rise to the common local perception that Geordie culture is somehow matriarchal. It is not that women hold the power outside the home, but that they are the focus of relationships within the family and have greater authority in this context than do fathers and grandfathers.

Ideas about family and motherhood are present in different ways in the teaching of the four churches. The role of Mary in the two Catholic churches has already been discussed at some length in Chapter 3. The women of both St Justin's and St Aidan's see in her a motherly presence within the divine, one who continues to mother them when their own mothers have died and a mother who can feel for them when they suffer at the hands of their children. However, it would be going too far to say that they see

Mary as a model for their own motherhood. Despite her ability to sympathise, she still appears too far removed from the reality of life to be a feasible model. The response of the women interviewed to the question of whether or not their relationship with Mary was different because of their own motherhood elicited only negative or indecisive responses. Indeed, when asked more generally if their Christianity had impacted on their way of mothering, the general response was very uncertain.

The churches themselves are not primarily places where families come together, except when occasional offices are being celebrated. Funerals, baptisms and the rarer weddings will gather families, bringing back members who have moved away,[31] but on regular Sundays, it is more often one member of the family who attends church, leaving the others behind. At church, there is little direct teaching about family roles. Neither the ministers of Green Memorial Methodist nor St Aidan's see this as a priority and the priest at St Justin's also preaches 'Kingdom values' rather than 'family values'. However, it is at St Justin's that members are most likely to find Church doctrine and private family matters overlapping in the Roman Catholic teaching on birth control and the Church's concern for the unborn child. Yet, even when the two worlds come together, it is not always the Church that wins the day:

> The only thing that got my goat, well it was a number of years ago, it was when my Alice was getting christened, she was only ten weeks old, . . . he [the priest] came across to the house, um, and said he'd rather, he'd like to have the christening at the Saturday night Easter vigil – at 12 o'clock at night. And I thought, well I've got one boy of four, one boy of two, . . . there is no way you can drag people out at that time of night, not with little children. And it was something I wanted the boys to be involved in. And he got quite uppity about it really. And I said, 'I'm sorry, Father, but you can't, you can't come into my house and tell me what I can do and what I can't do.[32]

Priests may have authority in the Church, but this does not extend into the realm of the home, where it is the mother who knows what is best for her family and will not accept outside interference, whatever the source. She, by defending the needs of her family and friends, is remaining closer to the central Christian ethic of care than the priest who is putting liturgy before people.

Motherhood brings authority as well as responsibility – it is a source of respect as well as of duties of care. Being a mother means having a recognised, central place in local society, as well as being at the beck and call of members of your immediate family. It is not a role that ends when the children leave home, but continues in the form of grandmothering and offering continued support, financial and otherwise, to adult offspring. In the next section, we will look at what feminist thought has to say about motherhood as a life role for women and what part it plays in the relationality debate.

The first thing that becomes clear from looking at feminist theology is that it has a somewhat ambivalent attitude to the relationship of motherhood. Mothering as giving life is seen to be a highly valuable and distinctive part of what it means to be a woman. At the same time, being defined by motherhood is seen as the epitome of the patriarchal labelling and dismissal of women. This is partly a reaction against the exaltation of motherhood as the only true fulfilment for women that is found in some traditional Church teaching, particularly, in more recent times at least, within the Roman Catholic Church. However, whether viewed positively or negatively – as quasi-divine creativity or as cage – motherhood still carries considerable emotional weight within feminist theology.

Black American womanist theologians have been among those who have argued most strenuously that mothering should be given positive attention. They point to the considerable role that mother-hood plays in the self-definition and self-worth of black women in America. As Dolores Williams says, 'for the womanist, mothering and nurturing are vitally important.'[33] The womanist emphasis is on mothering as a crucial part of the life experience of many women, white as well as black. However, they are also keen to emphasise that motherhood can be a very different experience for affluent white Americans, with the resources to provide a secure home for their children and pay for help in caring for them, than for poor, black women struggling to raise a family within the violent setting of an inner-city ghetto. The situation for black American women mirrors that described by Chung Hyun Kyung in her book *Struggle to be the Sun Again: Introducing Asian Women's Theology*.[34] In this she points out that, for Third World women, the struggle against multifaceted oppression must include men and children, because the struggle is too large for women alone and because men and children share many of their oppressions. Kyung emphasises that Asian women do their feminist theology as parts of embattled families rather than primarily as embattled individuals.

In Adrienne Rich's famous book *Of Woman Born: Motherhood as Institution and Experience*,[35] she expresses something of her own ambivalence towards her role as mother and, in so doing, reflects the unease felt by many other white feminist writers. Mothering for Rich offered both the strongest of joys – for example, the feeling when smelling the top of her babies' heads – and the strongest of frustrations – as she felt that her identity and creativity were sucked away in the demands of always caring for her children and husband. Some of the same discomfort is present in Paula M. Cooey's article 'Bad Women',[36] where she outlines the dangers of continuing the myth of the 'good mother'. In Cooey's eyes, 'being a good mother by definition precludes one from acting like a mature adult, subject to moral and emotional complexity.'[37] A 'good mother' can only be a woman who abandons her own needs and individuality in order to fulfil the needs of others and, by so doing, receives the praise of society. Any mother who puts her own needs on an equal basis with those of her family is demonised and dismissed as a 'bad mother'. So, for Cooey, one cannot be both a 'good mother', as defined by society, and a fulfilled human being.

One of the basic differences in approaches to motherhood between the women interviewed and feminist theologians, is that motherhood is, for the theologians, just one relationship within a whole pantheon of relationships. There is little sense that it has some form of priority or that its demands take precedence over other relationships or one's own self-fulfilment. In the lives of the Northern, working-class women I interviewed, motherhood is something much more than one chosen relationship among many. It is, rather, the relationship that is at the heart of their understanding of themselves and their place in their society. Motherhood, and daughterhood, is not a bar to discovering their full identity, but a central part of that very identity. Daughterhood, especially, is not a relationship that they have consciously chosen to give time and effort to, but one that has socially determined dimensions that appear entirely natural. This whole question of a relationship being a given, rather than a choice, will continue to be considered in the next section, in which the focus moves to eco-feminism and a relationality that stretches beyond the human to embrace the whole created order.

The natural world has not had a uniformly good press within Christianity. It has been identified with all that is contrary to the spiritual realm and the place of rebellion against God. Indeed, traditionally, we have prayed to be delivered from 'the world' and 'the flesh' as well as from 'the devil'. The resulting dualism, to which Greek philosophy also contributed, has already been mentioned as one of the particular bugbears of feminist theologians. They are not, it must be said, alone in their dislike of a system in which the material and bodily is devalued in order for the spiritual to be exalted. Eco-theologians – who are particularly concerned for the well-being of the planet – put part of the blame for our current ecological crisis on Christianity's lack of respect for non-human creation. They, along with the feminist writers, hope to see a change from the traditional devaluing of the material and a new sense of human kinship with all other living beings.

The particular input of feminist theologians, and the reason that many of them could be identified as eco-feminists, is their recognition that women are traditionally identified with the despised pole of the duality – alongside the material and bodily. This is seen to have paved the way for the justification of man's oppression of woman and humanity's uncontrolled use, and abuse, of natural resources. It has, therefore, seemed natural to many feminists to see the righting of patriarchal oppression of women as linked to the righting of the subjection of nature. Indeed, Rosemary Radford Ruether sees the one as being impossible without the other and speaks of the ultimate goal of a feminist vision being, 'a cultivation of the self that would be at one with an affirmation of others, both our immediate neighbours and all humanity and the Earth itself, as that "thou" with whom "I" am in a state of reciprocal interdependence.'[38]

Ruether's vision is largely shared by Sallie McFague, for whom the Earth can be seen as 'a tiny part of God's body'[39] – the visible reality of the invisible God. In her view, humanity's primary loyalty should not be to nation or to religion, but to the Earth and its Creator. We need to feel and know that we belong to the Earth in order for us to focus on the well-being of all, rather than the salvation of a few. In her exciting book *Life Abundant: Rethinking Theology and Economy for a Planet in Peril*,[40] McFague talks about the 'wild space' of God's kingdom as teaching us 'that *all* really are invited to the banquet, that every creature deserves a place at the table.'[41] Theology and spirituality are inseparable for McFague, from the conviction that human relationships and responsibility extend to all of the natural order – in her view, this is the fullest meaning of incarnation.[42]

Woman and nature are still seen to belong together in much feminist thought, but the value on each extreme of the pole has been reversed, so that both nature and the female are revered rather than despised. Our closeness to the rest of the created order is stressed, rather than downplayed, and the spiritual flourishing of humanity is seen to be intertwined with the physical flourishing of all forms of life on planet Earth. Even where the relationship between humanity and nature is believed to be equally relevant for men as well as women, it is still seen as part of the task of feminism to keep ecological needs at the forefront of theology, as the many 'eco-feminist' theologies show. Thus, relationality for many feminists does not refer merely to the interconnectedness of all humanity, but to the interconnectedness of all living beings – the 'web of life' as it is frequently named. Kathryn Tanner, for example, argues that we need to stress our shared creature-hood rather than our difference[43] and Melissa Raphael believes that the regeneration of female sacrality is intimately linked with the possibility of ecological regeneration.[44] In a similar spirit, the Asian theologians Chung Hyun Kyung and Kwok Pui-Lan see Asian women's spirituality as centring on creation and the inter-relatedness of all creatures, not just human beings. This characteristic is attributed by Kyung to the influence of Asian folk religion[45] and is summed up by Kwok Pui-Lan: 'For Asian feminist theologians spirituality is not so much a gaze toward heaven or an emptying of the self, but rather the celebration of *ki* (the energy of life), the joy of living and the quest for wholeness.'[46]

There is some argument about this identity of interest between women and nature, especially from womanist thinkers. Susan Thistlethwaite, for example, points out, 'white women have found in nature a sister and a source of reunification of the separations they experience as women; while black women have taken the conflicts of urban civilisation as their point of departure'.[47] Nature, in the experience of many black women, has not been an idyllic and romantic alternative to the city, but an opponent with which they have had to compete in order to drag a living from the ground. It is harder, in this context, to see human beings as in relationship with all other creatures and the Earth itself, especially as many black women are still struggling against the white culture's identification of them with the bestial and the non-human. It is more important for most womanists to emphasise the links between the oppression of black women and black men than between the oppression of black women and that of the natural world.

The womanist perspective is probably closest to that of the women in the interview group. There is not very much natural beauty within the Walker and Byker estates and the open spaces are often litter-strewn and spotted with dog dirt. It would not be true to say, however, that the natural world is entirely absent from the women's spirituality. When asked about places where they felt spiritual or found it natural to pray, there was some mention of walks in the countryside or looking out at gardens or the night sky:

> Um, I like country – I like the countryside. I like – at night sometimes I walk in the dark, you know, round here it's not very safe like. I like, um, the sky at night and the stars and everything, you know what I mean, that sort of helps me to think of, like, the greatness of God – the flowers and the country-side. (Susan, from St Justin's)

However, as in this quote, nature is more often seen as revealing the glory of its creator than being part of a web of connection with the women themselves. The closest they came to a sense of relationship with the created order was when Helen, from St Aidan's, asked about the fate of her dog after death and went on to say, 'Because I don't believe that they're soulless. Because what gives us the right to be the only ones with a soul?'

The similarity, in this case, is not that of eco-feminism, which emphasises our shared bodiliness, but a hope that animals, like people, contain an eternal part that will enable them to participate in life after death. Human beings are not recognising their shared creatureliness, but animals, or at least pets, are being lifted out of the natural world alongside us.

The centrality of this dualistic belief in body and soul will be seen in Chapter 6, when issues of death and the possibility of an afterlife are discussed. In that chapter also, the attitudes of the women interviewed to their bodies will be explored. However, it is important here to flag up the point that a bodily focus is not a natural one for these working-class women. They do not fit into the image of the body beautiful that wider society endorses. This is partly a result of age – they are all middle-aged or well beyond – and partly a result of the resources available to them. A 'body beautiful' – tall, slim, well-proportioned – begins with good childhood nutrition, which most of these women did not have. I have already mentioned that my five foot three inches seemed tall in local terms. Making a project of the body, by pampering and perfecting it, is also not a realistic option, calling as it does for resources of leisure time and money that they do not have available. Altogether, their bodies are not generally sources of self-worth or seen as contributing to their social value. Indeed, bodiliness for white, working-class, British women is, as for black, American women, too closely associated with their social denigration to be seen as a natural site of value and dignity.

It would be wrong, however, to regard the spirituality of these women as lacking in relationality – it is just that the direction of that relationship is very different. It has already been seen in Chapter 3 that, for many of the women, an intense romantic relationship with Jesus is at the centre of their faith and prayer life. This relationship is free from the mutual obligations and socially determined duties that accompany their familial ties and, instead, offers them unconditional affirmation. By means of this emotional connection with Jesus, their identity as spiritual beings, rather than mere animals, is reinforced and their sense of self-worth bolstered. A horizontal sense of relationship linking them to the rest of creation would not meet these needs nearly as satisfactorily as this vertical bond with the divine.[48]

The natural world is not really central to the lives of the women I interviewed. It is a source of pleasure and recreation – from holidays on Holy Island to watching the birds eat from the bird-feeder in the back garden – but it is not really more than this. When considered on a spiritual level, nature is seen as a source of wonder at the greatness of God and as inspiring prayer because of its beauty, but not as a partner in the spiritual process. There is no evidence for a sense of continuity of being between humanity and other forms of life, no potential for anything resembling a real relationship. The only exception to this is in the pets who may become 'members of the family', but they do so as honorary humans rather than as fellow animals. Neither women nor men are defined by creatureliness, nor would such a definition be seen as complimentary. To be like an animal is to be out of control, failing in respectability, it is not seen as being part of a sacred web of creation that deserves near-equal consideration with human interests.

There is no doubt that the concept of relationship is at the heart of feminist spirituality and theology. There is no precise definition of it – rather, it is used as a general corrective for a traditional patriarchal theology and spirituality that is judged to be destructively individualistic and far removed from the ethical imperative to care for others, including the planet Earth itself. To some, relationships are seen as the particular gift of women, while others would question its correlation with gender, but not its beneficial effects. Relationality is an unquestioned good for the majority of feminist theologians, although there are occasional voices reminding us of the need to be wary of its potential to keep women locked into patterns of care for others that do not allow them to develop their own potential and attend to their own needs.

The bonds of relationship in feminist thought are general rather than specific. They unite all people, making it impossible for spiritually aware Christians to consider their own salvation apart from the salvation, or flourishing, of all other people. Wider even than this, they tie us in to the entire web of life, which is made up of all living things that share our planet's biosphere. Spiritual maturity, in this context, means accepting the needs and rights of all living things – both because they have ultimate value in their own right and because our own survival and health are intimately connected with the survival and health of the planet as a whole. There is no end-point for our relationality, no place where we can say that we have come to the end of our responsibility to others, no 'others' who are outside the circle of our concern.

However, this theoretical universality can be hard to reconcile with the particularity that characterises real relationships. A relationality that embraces all of life can remain a purely abstract emotion, an idealised relationship that does not take into account the pulls and repulsions that are part of the emotional reality of face-to-face, year-by-year, encounter with the other. It is this pattern of emotional commitment and duty that we see in the relationships that shape the women on the local estates. There is nothing abstract about their interactions with family and neighbours and it would be true to say that these relationships play a larger part in the lives of most women than they do in the lives of most men. Ties of blood – especially the vertical relationships between grandparents, parents and children – have priority in terms of both emotional content and social obligation, but claims of neighbours and the wider community are also recognised. Compared to these grounded, and blood-based, connections, the relationality of feminist thought can seem somewhat anaemic.

These relationships do feed into the women's spirituality and their understanding of God, but not in the way that feminist thought idealises. Instead of bringing God down into the global web of interconnectedness, they bring to God the same loyalty and passion that marks their other relationships. God does not become the life force that powers all creativity and flourishing, but, rather, the perfect relationship, the one who gives the support and strength necessary if they are to keep their worldly relationships alive and healthy. God is the source of the unconditional love that allows them to meet the love with conditions and duties that their relatives and friends both give and demand. Meeting the needs of others is a concrete activity that makes it difficult to recognise obligations not embodied in the 'neighbour' – the other with whom one is personally acquainted. Wider relationships involve accepting the outsider – the asylum seeker, for example – within the scope of the community, rather than subscribing to a more abstract sense of the web of being.

The natural world impinges only peripherally on the spiritual lives of the women interviewed. It can be a source of wonder and the recognition of its beauty can inspire prayer. However, it remains a realm entirely separate from the human and there is no sense of continuity between women and men and all other living beings. Like the womanists in the United States, the women of the St Anthony's area are too aware of the need to differentiate themselves from the bestial, with which the wider community is prone to identify working-class females, to embrace the natural world too closely. Dogs and cats may be admitted into the community of relationships, but other animals remain outside it.

Relationships for the working-class women in this project are not things that you choose in order to enhance your spiritual life, but givens that you deal with as best you can. The concept of relationality would not be foreign to them – they know themselves, and others, by means of the matrix of relationship – but it would not be seen as something that is unquestionably positive. Relationships shape life for both good and ill, they are the source of the greatest joys and also of intense pain, and they severely limit the range of possibilities that are open to you. This applies first and foremost to the most intense of the relationships described – that between daughters and their mothers, and between mothers and their children of either sex. Feminist theologians seem to be accurate in their assessment that relationships are at the heart of women's experience of life, but they may have overstated their case in seeing this as both an undifferentiated and purely beneficial state of affairs. The reality of relationship is both messier, and more alive, than much feminist writing would lead us to believe.

Notes

1 Mary Grey, *The Wisdom of Fools? Seeking Revelation for Today*, London: SPCK, 1993, p. 59.
2 *The Religious Imagination of American Women*, Bloomington: Indiana University Press, 1999, p. 1.
3 *The Religious Imagination of American Women*, p. 3.

4 Judith Plaskow and Carol Christ (eds), *Weaving the Visions: New Patterns in Feminist Spirituality*, San Francisco: Harper & Row, 1989, p. 173.

5 M. H. Suchocki, 'God, sexism and transformation' in Rebecca Chopp and Mark Taylor (eds), *Reconstructing Christian Theology*, Minneapolis: Fortress, 1994, pp. 25–48.

6 *Prophecy and Mysticism: The Heart of the Postmodern Church*, Edinburgh: T. & T. Clark, 1997, p. 27, emphasis as in the original.

7 *Wisdom of Fools*, p. 99.

8 *Redeeming the Dream: Feminism, Redemption, and Christian Tradition*, London: SPCK, 1989, p. 126.

9 *Wisdom of Fools*, p. 129.

10 *In a Different Voice: Psychological Theory and Women's Development*, Cambridge, Massachusetts: Harvard University Press, 1982.

11 Such a brief synopsis inevitably entails caricaturing what are complicated and detailed theories that would need a book to themselves to be adequately explored.

12 Nancy Chodorow, 'Family structure and feminine personality' (1974) in Darlene M. Juschka (ed.), *Feminism in the Study of Religion: A Reader*, London: Continuum, 2001, p. 82.

13 'Family structure and feminine personality', p. 93.

14 *In a Different Voice*, p. 173.

15 The only real exception to this was Sheila, from St Aidan's. Her mother had been unmarried and this had caused her great pain as a child. She still does not talk about her childhood openly and prefers people not to know about her mother's situation.

16 Angela, from St Mark's. Angela's sister, Catherine, also spoke of her family in very warm terms.

17 Helen, from St Aidan's.

18 The question of whether or not the churches investigated were 'women's space' will be looked at much more fully in Chapter 5.

19 The single woman, Edith, was very proud of her work for the Foreign Office, which took her to London during World War II. She worked under the auspices of MI5 and had found it both thrilling and deeply satisfying. However, when she was demobbed, she immediately returned to the rest of the family in Newcastle.

20 *Religion in English Everyday Life: An Ethnographic Approach*, New York: Berghahn, 1999, p. 16.

21 *Women and Families: An Oral History, 1940–1970*, Oxford: Blackwell, 1995.

22 Marilyn Strathern, *After Nature: English Kinship in the Twentieth Century*, Cambridge: Cambridge University Press, 1992, p. 15.

23 See Strathern, *After Nature*, Chapter 1.

24 R. Firth, *Two Studies of Kinship in Britain*, London: Athone, 1956, quoted in the article by Justin McGlone, Alison Park and Ceridwen Roberts 'Kinship and friendship: attitudes and behavior in Britain 1986–1995' in Susan McRae (ed.), *Changing Britain: Families and Households in the 1990s*, Oxford: Oxford University Press, 1999, p. 141.

25 *The Family and Social Change: A Study of Family and Kinship in a South Wales Town*, London: Routledge & Kegan Paul, 1983.

26 See note 20.

27 *Religion in English Everyday Life*, p. 121.

28 *Religion in English Everyday Life*, p. 129.

29 *The Death of Christian Britain: Understanding Secularisation 1800–2000*, London and New York: Routledge, 2001.

30 *The Death of Christian Britain*, p. 195.

31 Baptisms, which are performed free by the church, are often considered expensive events as it is customary to mark them with a large party for family and friends. Often parents will wait and have all their children baptised together to save expense.

32 Ivy, from St Justin's.

33 From her article 'Womanist theology: black women's voices', pp. 179–86 of Judith Plaskow and Carol Christ (eds), *Weaving the Visions*, p. 183.

34 New York: Orbis, 1990.

35 London: Virago, 1976.

36 In Rebecca S. Chopp and Sheila Greeve Davaney (eds), *Horizons in Feminist Theology*, Minneapolis: Fortress, 1997, pp. 137–53.

37 'Bad Women' p. 143.

38 *New Woman, New Earth*, New York: Seabury, 1976, p. 211.

39 From her article 'Human beings, embodiment, and our home the Earth', in Rebecca S. Chopp and Mark Lewis Taylor (eds), *Reconstructing Christian Theology*, Minneapolis: Fortress, 1994, pp. 141–69.

40 Minneapolis: Fortress, 2001.

41 *Life Abundant*, p. 204, emphasis as in the original.

42 McFague's views on the immanent nature of divinity will be explored in the next chapter.

43 See her article 'Creation, environmental crisis, and ecological justice' in Chopp and Taylor, *Reconstructing Christian Theology*, pp. 99–123.

44 See Chapter 7 of *Thealogy and Embodiment: The Post-Patriarchal*

Reconstruction of Female Sacrality, Sheffield: Sheffield Academic Press, 1996.

45 See Chapter 6 of Chung Hyun Kyung, *Struggle to be the Sun Again: Introducing Asian Women's Theology*, New York: Orbis, 1990.

46 Kwok Pui-Lan, *Introducing Asian Feminist Theology*, Sheffield: Sheffield Academic Press, 2000, p. 114.

47 Susan Thistlethwaite, *Sex, Race and God: Christian Feminism in Black and White*, New York: Crossroad, 1989, p. 44.

48 The location of the divine in feminist theology and the spirituality of the interviewees will be discussed in detail in the following chapter.

5

'GOD'S PRESENCE IS THERE'

The intention of this chapter is to look at where God is located, both in contemporary feminist theology and the theology of the working-class women interviewed for this research. This involves two overlapping levels of enquiry. The first focuses on whether or not God is to be found within or outside the created universe, or, to use more technical language, the debate between transcendence and immanence as the preferred model for God. The second looks more closely at where God is experienced in the social world and looks at ideas and experiences of church in particular. As part of this discussion, it will be seen how each camp sees God's activity in the world: whether God is believed to be interventionist or remote from worldly concerns or absorbed into the natural processes of the world.

It has been apparent throughout this research that church is an important and special place for the women interviewed, which has played no small part in the development of their sense of religious self and their ideas about God. In this chapter, their involvement is looked at in more detail so it will be seen what they actually do in church, what they value about going, what irritates them about their church and if they feel that men and women should play different roles within the institution or not. Alongside this data is an analysis of feminist thought on the nature of church and how it can be a beneficial rather than oppressive space for women to worship in. Attention is paid to church as a potential space for horizontal relationships (person to person) to flourish, as well as a potential space for vertical relationships (person to God) to be experienced.

First of all, a brief explanation of the difference between pantheism and panentheism. Pantheism is the belief that the material universe is all that exists and, therefore, God has no existence outside material reality. This clearly rules out any belief in a transcendent God – one of the central tenets of Christianity. The little 'en' in panentheism is very important because this preserves a space for a transcendent God to exist. Unlike pantheism, panentheism teaches that the universe exists in God, but that God is still more than just the universe. To put it another way, in pantheism everything that is contains God, whereas in panentheism God contains everything that is.

The most notable feminist Christian pantheist is Grace Jantzen, who has already appeared in this book as an enemy of dualism. This enmity leads her not to atheism but to anti-theism – anti any idea of God that sees a separation between God and the world, between the spiritual and the material. Jantzen's anti-theism does not lead her to abandon the concept of God but radically redefine it. This redefinition leads directly to pantheism:

> If we took for granted that divinity – that which is most to be respected and valued – *means* mutuality, bodiliness, diversity, and materiality, then whether or not we believed that such a concept of God was instantiated, whether or not we clung to a realist stance, the implications for our thought and lives would be incalculable . . . instead of seeing domination as godlike we would recognise it as utterly contrary to divinity.[1]

As we already saw in Chapter 3, affirming this truth is more important to Jantzen than the question of whether or not 'such a concept of God was instantiated' – in other words, whether 'God' really exists or is simply the highest example of human imag(in)ing of the good. Again, it is the ethical motivation that is most important in Jantzen's thought.

One step back from Jantzen's position is that of such eco-feminists as Rosemary Radford Ruether and Sallie McFague, who embrace panentheism as opposed to Jantzen's pantheism. The difference between the two positions is clear in McFague's definition of panentheism: 'Everything that is is *in* God and God is *in* all things and yet God is not identical with the universe, for the universe is dependent on God in a way that God is not dependent on the universe.'[2] In McFague's book *Life Abundant*, which was mentioned in the last chapter, she continues to work with her earlier metaphor of the world as the body of God: 'Just as we are not primarily our bodies (though we are thoroughly bodily), so also God is not reduced to the body of the world but is also and primarily, the life and power, the breath and love, that make the universe what it is.'[3] Human selves and God are both embodied, but neither is completely defined by their body: each has a transcendent as well as an immanent aspect to their identity.

McFague's panentheism allows her to keep hold of the personal aspect of God that is essential if Christian eco-feminism is to remain truly Christian. She is, in fact, keeping the traditional two poles of Christian theological thought – that God is transcendent and that God is immanent – but changing the emphasis so that immanence rather than transcendence holds centre stage. There is no distance between God and the world, but, were the world to cease to exist, God would still be. McFague, like Jantzen, believes that the immanence of God provides the theological rationale for ethical activity focused on the good of the planet and all its inhabitants, but does not agree that retaining some concept of divine transcendence would undermine this ethical foundation. Indeed, *Life Abundant* is an attempt to unite theology and economic theory in order to provide a Christian ethical agenda for the wealthy West, the USA in particular. Jantzen and McFague share a sense of passion and urgency about the ethical task, though their theologies remain distinct.

Rosemary Radford Ruether treads a similar theological and ecological path to that of Sallie McFague. From her earliest book[4]

Ruether has linked the oppression of women to that of nature and seen feminist liberation as involving justice for the natural world as well as for women. Like Jantzen, this ecological interest has been matched and motivated by a desire to break down traditional dualities, although, like McFague, Ruether does not go as far as Jantzen towards pantheism. In *Gaia and God: An Ecofeminist Theology of Earth Healing*[5] Ruether is interested in reconciling Christianity and ecology, rather than making a theology from ecology. She attempts to answer the question she sets herself in the Introduction: 'Are Gaia, the living and sacred earth, and God, the monotheistic deity of the biblical traditions, on speaking terms with each other?'[6]

Although a great part of the book details ways in which traditional monotheistic Christianity has contributed to the sorry state of the planet today, Ruether does conclude by deciding that the voices of both Gaia and God need to be heard. God speaks the laws and commands that motivate urgent action, while Gaia 'speaks from the intimate heart of matter' in a voice that 'beckons us into communion'.[7] Ruether also says that both of these voices are our own. She does not mean that there is nothing beyond humanity or the world, as Jantzen might, but that it is only in human activity that these voices can be heard and their message acted on. The divine is immanent in the world as Gaia, but still is also transcendent. Human energy should be directed at creating abundant living for all creatures in this world, rather than aiming to find abundant life outside the material order, but the possibility of a life beyond the material is not ruled out.

I did not ask the question directly in the interviews – 'Where do you think God is?' – believing this too likely to provoke an orthodox response of 'everywhere', but the answers were apparent in material given in response to many of the other questions. It was there in the descriptions of their mental images of God, it was there when they talked about their spiritual life stories and the times when they had encountered, or felt abandoned by, God, and it was there in their beliefs about the process, and answering, of prayer. This section looks at the interviewees' sense of the location of God and, as an integral part of that sense, their understanding of God's interaction with this world.

The mental pictures of God have already been extensively discussed in Chapter 3. However, it is relevant to this argument to note certain characteristics about these images: those that play a role in placing God within the conceptual universe of the individual. There is obviously some difference here between the members of the Trinity. When describing God, most of the women talked of God the Father and Christ in distinctively different picture language, with the Holy Spirit getting a more occasional name check. Jesus Christ was, unsurprisingly, most often pictured in human terms as a person who, while being superior to all others, was still on a human scale and able to interact as a companion and fellow sufferer. He is both of and not of this world. God, as seen apart from Christ, appears either as an older, more distant, super person – the old man up in the heavens, or something more nebulous, expressed via abstract images and impressions of feelings. Into this category fall God as a comfy chair, God as the one who hugs and God as colour and light. These images place God within the realm of that which can be encountered and sensed, while remaining beyond full description and understanding.

God is portrayed as person or abstract, but, in both cases, he remains both immanent and transcendent. God can be encountered in the emotions and sensed as a personal presence, yet he is also outside the rules that govern the rest of the material universe. Encounter with God is something that can be talked of both in anthropomorphic terms and as belonging to the realm of the supernatural, set apart from all other forms of interpersonal encounter.

Encounters with God were talked about in response to my question 'Have you ever had anything you would call a spiritual experience?' The initial response was often to question what my understanding of 'spiritual experience' was. I tried to respond as generally as possible and to keep the ball in their court by saying that it could be anything that they thought of in this way.

Only four of the women said that they had never had such an experience – two of these went on to speak of what others might classify as spiritual experiences, Liz saying how God speaks directly to her via sermons and Ada mentioning that she did feel God's presence. The 15 women who were definite about having an encounter sometimes talked about experiences with deceased loved ones (these will be discussed in Chapter 6 when issues of death, finitude and eternity are addressed), but also of encounters with the divine. It is these that are examined next.

It is worth considering first the way in which the women spoke of these experiences as this begins to give an insight into the experiences' salience within their wider lives. The only hesitation the women displayed was in asking for clarification of what a 'spiritual experience' might be considered to be. When they felt that their experience wouldn't be discounted, they spoke of it with no further delay. It was common at this point for the tempo of the voice to slow slightly, as a reflective, thoughtful note came into it. The stories were told as if they were precious to the teller and were entrusted to the listener as something of great worth that was to be taken seriously. I didn't get the impression that these were stories that they repeated to many people, but there was a sense that they had been often told to themselves. It must also be said that some of the women recounted the events in voices that changed not at all, as if they were an expected and almost commonplace part of life.

The woman who spoke of her spiritual experience with the most emotion, tears coming into her eyes as she talked, was Susan, from St Justin's. Her experience was very different from most of those described, both in its nature and in its effects on her subsequent life. She describes it as a vivid dream in which a weeping Christ told her that she was piercing his heart with her lack of love for him and it ended with the command, 'Well, if you're really sorry then come and find me.' This dream was followed in the next few days by a continued state of spiritual intensity:

this overwhelming presence came. And I was so frightened – I was – I just couldn't – I thought this is too, like, real, you know . . . what's happening to us? And I thought, I came to the conclusion, that it was either . . . I was going to die . . . or I'm going to be a saint.

The fear in this experience came from the feeling that God was 'too real', too present in this world, when God would normally be expected to be safely distant. It was almost an invasion of Susan's space, a condition that she described as continuing for 'months and months' and resulting in her feeling isolated and lonely. The senses of both love and guilt were poignantly real for her and, in her own eyes, set her apart from her teenage contemporaries. The whole experience has led her to make her spiritual journey the focus of her life's work and meant that she did consider joining a religious order before her poor health ruled this out.

After a few months, the intensity of the sensation wore away and Susan spoke of the presence of God in terms of comfort and help – the sort of language that most of the women used when describing God's presence. In most cases, spiritual experiences did not come as calls for transformation, but as consolation and affirmation. They offered paternal comfort and companionship rather than a challenge to change. God's presence was, indeed, more frequently remarked on at times of sadness and loss. The words of Ruth, from Green Memorial Methodist, are typical:

I suppose it is a cliché, but when the times are hard you definitely feel God's presence more. I don't know if it's because you're aware of it and you're looking for it, but it is there.

The terms in which this presence are described are those of comfort – being surrounded by a sense of love and warmth, feeling less lonely, finding yourself at peace or, in Catherine's words:

I've always felt that I'm a protected species, and the protection is his arms around me. I can always conjure up the feeling – which I can at this minute now – that there's two arms around me just holding me, and it's wonderful.

This very physical image was not particularly typical – often what was described was the knowledge, or a sense, that God was in some way there with them. This was often mentioned in connection with worship – the feeling that God was particularly present within the building[8] – or in connection with prayer, when there was the conviction that there was somebody listening to what was being said. Angela, from St Mark's, did want to emphasise that God was with her during the good times as well as the bad:

I think when you're enjoying good times as well, I think you can feel that God is there cheering you on. Um, and even just sometimes little things, you know, you'll set out for a day, just to go for a day out, and really you feel that God's with you.

This is a God whose presence is natural rather than overwhelming, a friend wanting to share and increase a sense of happiness and well-being.

There were other spiritual experiences that had more dramatic and visionary manifestations. Marie, the member of St Justin's whose passionate love for Jesus was described in Chapter 3, was also very aware of the presence of the Virgin Mary: 'And, um, I was like, I mean, little pictures and visions and things where she would come close to us.'

Monica, another Roman Catholic, had the experience of seeing a picture of Jesus on the white wafer, the host, displayed in the monstrance,[9] while, as we saw earlier, an Anglo-Catholic, Rose, felt her wheelchair being gently rocked by the Virgin Mary when visiting Walsingham. In all cases, these experiences were highly prized, though the women did not feel confident in talking about them to many people. They were felt to be outside the normal order of things and to bring with them the risk of the accusation of insanity. To quote Marie again:

> Well, before that you know people kind of think you're strange. When, you know, from no religion and all of a sudden you change, you know. They can't understand it, you know. And I used to say to Our Lady, 'Well, if I am going daft, it's a lovely way to go draft!' I used to say, 'It is lovely if this is the way you lose your mind', you know!

Sensory religious experiences are both a privilege and a risk, bringing with them the sense of having moved outside the ordinary, rational world.

There is not space in this book to look into the psychological and sociological aspects of the phenomenon of spiritual experiences such as these, nor is it directly relevant to this project. The purpose of the interest in the religious experiences here is what they tell us about the normal expectations of the location of God, which are thrown into relief by the extraordinary nature of these encounters. You do not normally expect to meet God so directly in this world. Seeing God's face and hearing God's voice or speaking with the saints are events that are normally reserved for the next life. When these experiences do occur, there is a definite sense of one realm breaking into the other, which can only be explained by ideas of imminent death or imminent sanctification or by the worldly explanation of imminent insanity. The transcendent God is not supposed to be met directly within our world, but to be at a distance from the everyday.

This is not to say that God leaves no traces of Godself within this world. The women interviewed expected to feel the presence of God at certain times, especially when they were in pain of some sort, though they were also not surprised by periods when they were not aware of God being with them. The closeness when it came was comforting and reassuring, but usually quite abstract – a diffused feeling of 'peace' and 'love'. What is particularly interesting is that these sensations remained firmly within the interpersonal – they were emotions that might be experienced in close human relationships. None of the women described a spiritual experience of being at one with all other living things, being caught up into a union with all life, divine and created. Divinity is not, in their experience, 'at home' in this world, although encounter is possible. Divinity is 'at home' in another realm, from where it can make its presence felt in this one. In more academic language, God is primarily, though not exclusively, transcendent and not primarily immanent.

There is, however, one way in which these spiritual experiences do fit within a feminist interpretation of spirituality. Apart perhaps from Susan's, they are not experiences that call the women away from their place in family and society, but, rather, affirm their value in their current location. They are not experiences of transformation but of affirmation. The women remain within the relationships of family and community, which are in no way undermined by their individual encounters with the divine. Their God may be transcendent rather than immanent, but he respects human relationships and does not demand that all other ties be abandoned in his service.

It is also possible to discover where God is placed by examining the way that the women talked about how they prayed – in particular, their expectations of being listened to and answered. This section will look at what they had to say about their private prayer, as communal worship will be considered later in the chapter. It will be seen where their prayers were directed and how they understood God's activity in the world.

All the women did say that they tried to pray during the week, though many of them admitted that they found this difficult to do.[10] They most often spoke of praying first thing in the morning or just before going to bed at night – at either of these times they might actually pray while lying in bed. Also mentioned were prayers during the day in reaction either to bad news on the TV or because of their own immediate need for help. Both forms of prayer were often felt to be an essential coping mechanism, as Monica, from St Justin's, says, 'I couldn't get by without my daily prayer. I know that I couldn't just sort of function and get from A to B, you know.'

Prayer isn't only for the important things but for any activity where help is felt to be needed:

> I do little prayers through the day, shall we say. Silly little prayers sometimes. If you're baking a cake for a special occasion, I've been known to say, 'Oh please, God, let this cake be nice.' (Angela, from St Mark's)

For some of the women, their prayer amounts to a daily conversation with God or Jesus in which all the day's pleasures and frustrations are shared, thanks being given and help asked for as appropriate.

The God to whom the women pray is one who is always available and willing to listen. He is available not because he shares the natural world with humanity, but because he is outside the natural order and, therefore, accessible to all people at all times. The women, when not using the simple term 'God', spoke most often of praying either to the Father or to Jesus, though the Catholic women also mentioned Mary in this context. They are not treated as distant figures, but as familiar friends who have the women's best interests at heart. They are also powerful: the women expect to have their prayers answered and cite examples of when this has happened. In response to the question, 'And have you felt that your prayers are answered?', Enid, from St Justin's, replied:

> Oh, often, often. Just Wednesday morning, I had asked our Blessed Lady to send somebody to us and . . . When this person arrived and said, 'I can give you a lift' . . . you know when he got into the car he said, 'I bet your prayers have been answered.' And was that not proof of what I'm saying to you?

God, directly or through the persons of Mary or Jesus is able to intervene in the world and reorder it so that it better suits those who have the faith and who ask God properly.

The women did not only speak of their own prayers being answered, but also mentioned times when they or members of their family had been the subjects of other people's prayers. This was usually at times of crisis or illness. Vera, from St Justin's, talked about the time that her husband was critically ill with cancer and had many people praying for him:[11]

> And, do you know, I couldn't believe it, after a few weeks went by he had to go into hospital to see what was what and the tumour had gone! . . . So that I'm sure prayers were answered there. I'm sure of it.

Vera's husband had been undergoing medical treatment so they were not relying solely on the power of prayer. In a similar situation, when her son was critically injured in a motorcycle accident, Angela, from St Mark's, also talked about the power of many people praying together. She is convinced that God still works miracles today:

> Miracles do happen today, but they don't in a flash, you know. Because I think doctors and surgeons and what have you are working miracles and, to me, God is working through these people.

God's intervention is at one remove here as God is working through human agents rather than intervening directly. This speaks again of the women's sense of God's distance from the natural world as much as for their belief in God's particular care for them and ability to influence the outcome of events.

Just as there were times when individual women spoke of their awareness of periods of God's absence, so also some spoke of prayers that hadn't been answered. Sarah, from St Aidan's, felt that she had only had 'half her prayers answered' and still continued to pray that her daughter and grandson might be reconciled. Anna, also from St Aidan's, was confused and distressed because God did not seem to be responding to her pleas to have her two sons reconciled:

And I pray, I pray for that. That is the only thing that sticks in my mind, why I can't have this prayer answered, you know. 'Cos I pray all the time and it never leaves my mind, never.

This was said with tears gathering in her eyes and ended with an appeal to me to explain it to her. She obviously felt that it was well within God's power to answer her prayer and could not understand why he should be making her suffer by refusing to do what she asked. It was clear that the blame lay with God or herself for failing as a mother, rather than with her two feuding sons.

The God to whom the women pray is not in the same room with them, nor in the same world. However, neither is God inaccessible or uninterested in the minutiae of the lives of his people. He is able to intervene and the expectation is that he will be willing to do so, though contemporary miracles may rely on the efforts of human beings rather than the direct action of the finger of God. God is worth praying to exactly because he does transcend the limitations of finite existence and can alter the laws of nature – human or organic – should he be persuaded that this is necessary. However, this transcendent God is not an uninvolved God. He is incarnate in the actions of medical professionals and feels deeply for all the everyday triumphs and heartaches of the women. In a strange paradox, God is never closer to the women than when he is recognised as most different from them. It is when he acts out of his paternal care that they feel most assured of being loved and valued and that their powerlessness is not complete.

It is time to move from questions of immanence and transcendence, of where God is to be found within the cosmos, to look at where God is to be encountered in daily social life. This, in view

of the importance attached to it both by the women interviewed
and (positively and negatively) by feminist theologians, will mean
looking in particular at the place of the Church.

> Just as secular feminism has often made women feel guilty for
> having husbands, so feminist theology has often made women
> feel guilty for believing in the incarnation or resurrection, or
> for valuing the Church.[12]

The Church has been a much debated subject within feminist
theology, the focus of much pointed criticism as well as suggestions
for how it is to be redeemed. This section focuses on the work
of two feminist theologians who have written both critically and
idealistically about the Church: Mary Grey, from the perspective
of the UK, and Letty Russell, from the perspective of the USA.
Both believe that there are serious flaws in the Church as it is and
have various suggestions for how these could be corrected. Between
them, they can only give a partial image of the full spectrum of
feminist work in this field, but they do provide an interesting
glimpse of it.[13]

It's no surprise, from what we have seen of her work already,
that Mary Grey puts relationships and community at the heart of
her ideal of the Church. In *The Wisdom of Fools? Seeking Revelation
for Today*,[14] she describes what she believes to be the essential
elements of a feminist vision of the Church: 'Solidarity, mutuality,
interdependence and commitment to the ongoing process of liberation are the very foundations of feminist Christian community.'[15]
Grey sees these qualities as springing from a new openness to the
Spirit of God, which brings connection and breaks down the barriers of individualism and separation. Patriarchal hierarchy is the
enemy of this new way of being Church because it puts barriers
between people and between the Spirit and the people.

Unlike some more radical feminist writers, Grey does not advocate an exodus from existing Church structures, however deeply
flawed they may be. Instead, she wants to see these structures

changed and the Church saved from itself. This salvation lies in the Church becoming a true mirror of both human and divine reality, which, Grey firmly believes, is relationality. The doctrine of the Trinity teaches that relationship is at the heart of God's very self, while the human person's intrinsic need for relationships means that they can only flourish within the context of a community.[16] It is, therefore, only a Church based on relationality and community that can echo divine reality and meet basic human needs. This does not mean for Grey that the Church should seek to be a homogenous community in which all people are seen as essentially the same. Instead, in tune with present feminist orthodoxies, she values difference as well as connection; 'otherness' remains while division is at an end. What does come through in all Grey's writing on the subject is an overwhelming concern with the horizontal relationships that make up the Church and far less interest in the vertical dimension of worship. The impression you get from reading her work is that the business of the Church is primarily the building of community rather than the worship of God – or, perhaps, that building community *is* the most acceptable way to worship God.

A similar critique of the traditional Church as exclusive and hierarchical can be found in the work of Letty Russell, as well as, it must be said, the vast majority of feminist and liberationist writers on the subject. Indeed, the very title of Russell's major book signals her view of the shape the Church should take if it is to embody feminist insights: *Church in the Round: Feminist Interpretation of the Church*.[17] Russell uses the images of two tables to symbolise her vision for the Church, stating that, '*The critical principle of feminist ecclesiology is a table principle*.'[18] The round table – freed from its association with heroic myth and kingly power – is a symbol of inclusivity and the sharing of power and authority. The kitchen table is a symbol of the Church as a place embedded in the necessities and practicalities of life, a place where work is to be done and where change can take place. Both these tables need to be open to all people and not hedged around by protective decrees. Indeed, Russell questions the value of her own ordination because that can be seen to set some members of the table fellowship apart from the rest of the community. Power and authority are not concepts with which Russell is comfortable.

In Russell's Church, like Grey's, there are more important things to talk about than worship. Tables are a place for the gathering of the people rather than a site for the offering of a spiritual sacrifice to God, and encounter with God only comes about via encounter with the other sisters and brothers in the circle of the Church community. In Russell's view, it is right action – which means action for justice and a move towards the margins of society – that should define the Church rather then its doctrine or its worship practices. The overall impression from the book is that the Church needs to be a *doing* community rather than a *worshipping* community. It is a place where the Kingdom values of openness, justice and hospitality ought to be practised and where individuals put aside their self-interest in favour of seeking communal well-being for all people on the planet. It is in this activity and connectedness that true spirituality is to be found, rather than in any individual's connection with a transcendent God.

Russell and Grey both speak out of the mainstream of feminist Christian orthodoxy about the proper role of the Church within Christianity. It is to be a place where Christians encounter one another as equals and in which all experience, especially that of women and other marginalised groups, is heard and valued. Its primary role is to be a place of community and relationality where doors are always open, barriers are broken down and power is shared – a foretaste of the feminist kingdom of God. Worship will take place there, but the assumption seems to be that this will flow naturally from the renewed community and need not be the subject of feminist discussion now.[19] The old Church, with its hierarchical structure and emphasis on personal devotion, is seen as a counter-productive environment for the true flourishing of female Christians, especially in light of the exclusion of women from positions of power. A feminist Church will be the opposite of what has gone before and, in its difference, will provide the necessary soil for female and male flourishing, communal more than individual, in the image of a relational God.

It will be remembered that four churches were included in this study: one Roman Catholic, one Methodist, one evangelical Anglican and one Anglo-Catholic.[20] All are within a short distance of one another and, therefore, a short distance from the vicarage of the high Anglican parish in which I live. In this section, I first of all look at the interview data on how the women experienced their particular church, with both its positive and negative aspects being considered. In the next section, this information is augmented by some of the sociological insights into church attendance.

All the women interviewed, with just one exception,[21] were closely involved with the life of their respective church and, sometimes, with the wider ecumenical life of the area. They were all long-term church members, although most had had periods of their lives when they did not attend. This was often the period between attending Sunday school and having families of their own. For some, it took a particular event to bring them into church. For Liz, this was a personal tragedy:

I always felt part of the church because I was part of the school, but I never went to church until the baby died. I'd always wanted to go back, but I just never did – I was too involved in my own life.[22]

In other cases, the women returned because they were invited by existing members of the congregation. This was a way of moving past the embarrassment of being seen as a backslider. In all the churches, the numbers attending had steadily, and quite drastically, declined over the last 50 years (a phenomenon that will be looked at more closely later in this chapter when the sociology of church-going is considered), but the women interviewed displayed great loyalty and love towards their particular church:

I love that church down there, I absolutely love it. (Anna, from St Aidan's)

I don't think anybody would stop us going to church because it's a big part of my life. I love going, I do, I love going, you get lovely feelings. (Tracy, from St Justin's)

I would feel as if I didn't exist, sort of, if I didn't go to church. (Ada, from St Mark's)

The women all did various jobs within the services of their various denominations and some had duties during the week. They read lessons, led intercessions, served at the altar, chose the hymns, took the sacrament to the housebound, sat on church councils, acted as treasurer, helped with the cleaning and some even arranged the flowers. Of all these activities, it was the ones during the services that were most important to them – both in offering a sense of privilege and involvement and in being the most nerve-wracking to do. Only one of the women spoke of a wish to do more in church. Monica, from St Justin's, felt that she might explore a calling to the ordained ministry if such a thing were ever allowed within the Roman Catholic Church. Otherwise, there was a sense that the women were already as involved as they would choose to be, although there were differing views about whether or not women in general should be allowed to take on the roles that were currently exclusively male preserves.[23]

I asked the women what it was about their church that kept them going or what it was that they liked best about the experience of being there. Their answers fell into two camps. Either they mentioned the worship as being key or they talked of the people as being the most important motivator. For some of them, it was hard to distinguish any one particular element that made churchgoing a good experience and, instead, they talked about the way that church made them feel, using terms such as 'lovely', 'calm', 'safe' and 'nice'. Being inside that particular building with all its associations was important. Even when they accepted that God was everywhere, there was still felt to be something special about that particular space, as Angela, from St Mark's, expressed most clearly: 'The feeling of God's presence the moment you walk in. I know God's with us all the time, but, you know, God's presence is there.'

The value placed by the congregations on the buildings is evidenced by the care with which they are looked after[24] and the anger that is felt when they are vandalised. It is the same care and anger that women express about their own homes, suggesting that their church is in some way a spiritual home from home – a place of their own that they need to look after and others should respect.

The women who felt that it was some part of the worship that was most important in keeping them attending church found different parts of the service most significant. For one it was the hymns, for another the Bible teaching,[25] but for most it was a closeness to God that only came when worshipping in church. This closeness was frequently associated with the Eucharist and, in the Anglo-Catholic and Roman Catholic churches, the act of receiving the sacrament. This is how Enid, from St Justin's, spoke of that moment:

> You know you hear people saying, 'Well, there's God inside everybody?' Well, I know there is without even receiving, but you actually, when you receive, you get that, that warmth and glow that gives you strength. Lovely. I love it.

This receiving of the sacrament is the ultimate moment of closeness between the individual woman and her God – the other members of the congregation are not significant at this high point as the focus is exclusively vertical. It is this vertical relationship that is the point of going to church for many. Close relationships with other people are available elsewhere, but this closeness with God is particular to being in church. Receiving God in 'the body and the blood' reinforces the connection between God and the individual like no other single event and, while it happens in the context of communal worship, is still a deeply personal and private affair.

As mentioned above, there are others for whom the human contact at church is important. This is expressed most strongly by Catherine, from St Mark's:

> What keeps me part of it is the fellowship, and I suppose it's been feeling part of a family. That there are people you've grown together, you're on a journey together and you become used to them. I think there's a bond of love there, and that's what keeps me going.

Others also mentioned the benefits they received from being with people who were making the same spiritual journey and the help it was to feel that you were not alone in trying to worship God. Liz, from St Aidan's, spoke both about how 'comfortable' she felt being with other people who wanted to worship but also stressed that she didn't 'need the community of the church'. There wasn't the sense that the church provided the only, or necessarily the primary, community in these women's lives. They were rooted in their family and their neighbourhood and had no perceptible feeling of isolation that churchgoing compensated for. Church was shared with the same people who shared the rest of everyday life, which kept the experience rooted in reality as well as connecting with the supernatural: 'You get all the "grumpies" and you get all the "happies", a real mixture, and it sort of brings you back down to Earth.'[26]

The other people at church were not viewed as an unalloyed blessing. When asked what irritated them about church, the women often referred to the level of chatter and noise that interrupted their personal devotions. In some cases, children were seen as being particularly disruptive, though the women often felt a bit guilty about saying this. There was also annoyance with the petty bickering that could mark the community, with people being ready to take offence at the slightest thing. In other cases, the irritations came from the failure of the Church as an institution. One person mentioned that the Church (Anglican in this case) was too intellectual and talked over people's heads, while Susan, from St Justin's, was very concerned about the Church's attitude to money. She cites the cost of retreats as an example and goes on to say how much she would hate it if the Church were to become 'middle-class'. No mention was made of the hierarchical structure of the Church being a problem or the role that it assigns to women. That not everyone agreed with their own church's policies in these matters became clear in response to other questions, but they did not spring to mind as aspects of church life that were frustrating on a daily basis.

Church, for the women interviewed, is a place where they go to be closer to God and, for some of them, to be closer to their neighbours. It is an intrinsic part of their lives – essential for their spiritual nourishment and a central part of their self-identity. This self-identity involves seeing themselves as having a personal relationship with God, focused for many on the reception of the Eucharistic elements, and being people who worship and pray. This identity also influences their sense of standing within the wider community, as Liz, from St Aidan's, says:

> It's nice that you do go to church, because if somebody else has a problem they'll approach you because you are a member of the church, which is nice. I like to be seen in the community as somebody who goes to church.

However, although their place in the community might be influenced by attending church, church itself is not essential to provide them with a community. The affirmation of their relationship with God predominates over any human relationships in their perception of the value of churchgoing. Church is seen as a place for the vertical link with God as much, and more often more, than the horizontal link with other human beings.

The horizontal relationships within church communities are very predominantly relationships between women. The vast majority of each church congregation is female – a situation of which the women are very aware and about which they feel a certain amount of dismay. In this section, I will look at the women's thoughts about the different roles of women and men within the Church and the reasons they gave for it having become (or having always been) 'women's space'.

The women all knew that they were being interviewed by a woman priest and this may have influenced the answers they gave to questions about the role of women in the Church. However, as I mentioned in Chapter 1, it did not seem that this happened to a great extent, the women on the whole being used to plain speaking. It was interesting that this was one of the areas where there were some clear divisions between the four congregations. Of the four churches, only the Methodists had had any direct experience of a woman minister; the other three were all officially against women priests. None of the Methodists interviewed saw any difference between women and men leading congregations, though some did feel that it had been harder for women to be accepted in this role. The Roman Catholic and Anglo-Catholic women varied in their thinking about the validity of women priests, while the evangelical Anglicans were unanimous in their rejection of women taking on such a leadership position.

Those who did not approve of women priests among the Roman and Anglo-Catholics, tended to say that it just wouldn't feel right to receive Communion from a woman. Anna, an Anglican who would like to have women priests because they would be easier to talk to, went on to say, 'But when it comes to Communion, for some reason, I think it's better given by a man.'

When reasons were given for preferring male priests – as they were by the evangelical Anglicans – they centred on the different roles that God had created men and women for. In Catherine's words:

He created us male and female for a purpose ... I think we're complementary one to another. I think there are roles that men can do and roles that women can do. Um, and I think leadership I see mainly as a male role, and that's what I see in a priest is a leader, and I feel that is a male role.

None of the women felt that her role was less important than a man's or that women were inferior to men, but they did insist on the need for distinction and difference between the sexes. For some of the Catholic women, there was a distinct welcome given to the idea of women priests, partly on the grounds that women are different and so would bring different gifts and partly on the grounds of our equality in the eyes of God: 'I don't think God sees wer as men and women. I think he sees wer as his family, his children, you know. You know I can't see any difference at all.'[27]

The issue of only having male priests was not a burning one for any of the women who were open to women in the role, with the possible exception of Monica, from St Justin's, but it is interesting to see how far they were from the official Church thinking on this matter.

The women were quite clear about why the church pews were full of women rather than men. The put it down to a traditional North-Eastern working-class perception that 'praying was women's work', as Catherine phrased it. This was believed to be part of the macho culture of the estates and a particularly working-class phenomenon:

Um, but I think it's just, I think it's just working men, just don't want to appear – it's my opinion – they just don't want to appear soft and think – hm, it's going to church, you know, it's a religious – I mean, or somebody will skit them about it, you know. (Rose, from St Aidan's)

None of the women seemed to be content that churches should be women's spaces so exclusively. Indeed, there was a general feeling that a more equal balance between the sexes would be an improvement. Some also talked about times in which the situation had been very different. Particularly at St Aidan's, the congregation referred back to a golden age (vaguely dated to the 1950s) when the shipyard men used to attend an early mass each morning before starting work. Even in this scenario, however, the impression is not of women and men sharing church space, but of them occupying it at different times. There is no perceived solution to the problem, just a sense that it is a vicious circle and that, while men see only women in church, they will not commit to it themselves.

The comments of one of the members of the Green Memorial Methodist congregation make an interesting bridge between this section and the next, which will look briefly at some of the sociology of church attendance. Ruth, a teacher, sees going to church as a duty that is an extension of her working life. She is quite critical of traditional 'churchiness', having, as a teenager, shocked her mother by saying that Jesus would be 'under the Tyne bridge with the homeless people' rather than inside a church, but she is also clear that it is the change in women's roles within society that has brought about the Church's decline:

> I think the women have kept the churches going and I think women who work now have played a great part in the downfall of the Church. Because they're not there to keep things going through the day, they're not there to do the fundraising, they can't take an active quiet part. Because in the old days they used to keep the Church running, the men were figureheads. We haven't even got figureheads now as men, but we haven't got the women quietly beavering away in the background and I think the change in society has changed a lot in the churches.

Church as 'woman's space' will fail if women do not put in sufficient time and energy to maintain it and, in Ruth's opinion, this is the most likely outcome of the new commitment of women to careers outside the home.

It is not my intention in this section to offer a minimalist overview of the sociology of church attendance, but to look at one work, mentioned in Chapter 4, that echoes the concerns Ruth mentioned above. This is Callum G. Brown's book *The Death of Christian Britain: Understanding Secularisation 1800–2000*.[28] Brown's basic thesis on the process of secularisation is very similar to Ruth's explanation for the decline in church attendance in the North East:

> The book focuses considerable attention on how piety was conceived as an overwhelmingly feminine trait which challenged masculinity and left men demonised and constantly anxious . . . As a result, women, rather than cities or social class, emerge as the principal source of explanation for the patterns of religiosity that were observable in the nineteenth and twentieth centuries. Most importantly, two other things will emerge. First, women were the bulwark to popular support for organised Christianity between 1800 and 1963, and second it was they who broke their relationship to Christian piety in the 1960s and thereby caused secularisation.[29]

Women are the key to the decline in church attendance for Callum Brown and for Ruth because they both believe that women were the ones who kept the churches flourishing during previous generations.

Brown sees the beginning of the feminisation of religion occurring in the early nineteenth century as piety began to be seen as a gentle, womanly virtue rather than a heroic and manly one. Women became more closely identified with the domestic sphere and gained value in their role as 'angels of the home' – providing men with a refuge and sanctuary (the religious overtones are appropriate) from the rough and tumble of the public world. The moral tone of the family, and so of the nation, was the responsibility of wives and mothers, who gained respectability only via their moral virtue, primarily evidenced to the world by their churchgoing and the cleanliness of their families and homes.[30] Brown is not particularly clear about whether or not this connection was attenuated during the World Wars, when women were very active outside the home, but does see it as being reinforced by the renewed domesticity of the 1950s. It only came to an end, in his view, when the new youth culture of the 1960s offered women more alternatives, with the goods of choice and liberalisation replacing the imperative to be respectable.

This leads Brown to the point where he considers the place of the Church in British society today. He still sees churches as primarily female enclaves, but ones that have become irrelevant to all but the older generation:

> Women still make up the majority of churchgoers. But they are overwhelmingly older women, raised under the old discourses, and who continue to seek affirmation of their moral and feminine identities in the Christian church. Men are proportionately under-represented as they always have been, but then Sunday church service is still an 'unmanly' site in discourse. The really important group that is missing from church is young women and girls.[31]

At first sight, this may seem to be an accurate reflection of the situation of the four churches in this study. None of the women is accompanied to church by her daughters or her sons, although sometimes some do take their grandchildren with them. When asked about whether or not their children are churchgoers, the answers were varied. Some were, but in a different part of the region or the country, others had been but had now stopped, while some attended very occasionally. As has already been mentioned, the fact that the ages of my interviewees ranged from their forties to their eighties reflected the reality of the age weighting in the local congregations.

However, there are two areas where the data in my research conflict with those of Callum Brown. The first is that, for a considerable number of these women, churchgoing has not always been a part of their lives. They did not seem to find church attendance a necessary part of respectability when they were in their late teens or looking after young families, which is one reason for them being sanguine about the possibility of their children coming back to church later in life. Their choice of church has not been because it is the only discourse that makes sense to them as women who grew up before the changes of the 1960s, but because it contributes to their life where they are now. It is, of course, easier for them to feel at home there because they are among people who are like themselves – older women – and there is no doubt that this attendance profile does not attract younger and/or male members.

The second area of data that is at odds with Brown's conclusions is the motivation that brings women in to their church and makes them decide each Sunday that it is worth continuing to go. Brown's sociological perspective leaves little room for individual choice or for the psychological reality and importance of spiritual experience. His religion is one of morality and outward observance, with no space for the experience of the transcendent. This may be right and proper for a sociologist, but it would be wrong in my method of research to discount the self-understanding of my interviewees in favour of an academic theory. This is not to deny that the women I interviewed are, as we all are, subject to social determinants that may be outside their conscious perception, but it is to assert that such determinants are only part of the whole picture.

The reasons for these women going to church are complicated and multilayered. They have something to do with the expectations of female behaviour in local culture, but they also have to do with the value that the women place individually on the experience of churchgoing. This value is primarily to do with it reinforcing their sense of personal communion with God, with its attendant benefits for their sense of self-worth, rather than with it validating their worth in the eyes of others. It may be that churchgoing does not perform this same role for their daughters or sons, although, as Grace Davie points out in *Religion in Britain Since 1945: Believing Without Belonging*,[32] it is still difficult to tell if we are 'experiencing a marked *generational* shift with respect to religious behaviour, or are the variations so far indicated simply in accordance with the normal manifestations of the lifecycle?'[33] It cannot be denied that age plays a pronounced role along with gender in determining who attends church, but it is less certain why this is so and what it tells us about the likely future of organised Christianity in Britain.

The majority of writers of feminist theology are very clear about where God is to be found and where God should not be looked for. God is here in this world, found in the relationships that bind people and all forms of life into one continuum – Gaia is – at least part of – God. While most within the Christian tradition of feminist thought would want to keep a panentheistic, rather than pantheistic, outlook, they would still emphasise that to look for God within the transcendent realm is to somehow miss the point. God is to be experienced via God's creation and worshipped in the service of this creation. God's immanence is of central importance, God's transcendence is (usually) acknowledged but then dismissed as irrelevant, or inimical, to ethical practice. This emphasis is continued in feminist ideas about the nature of the Church and, particularly, their pictures of what a woman-friendly Church would look like. It would be a community without hierarchy, open and welcoming to all varieties of people and focused on ethical action for the improvement of the quality of life for all inhabiting the Earth. Its characteristic relationship would be the horizontal bond of sisterhood and brotherhood rather than the vertical bond of individual worshipper to his or her God.

It is immediately clear that the women in this study look for God in different places and find in churchgoing a different utility from that suggested by feminist writers. God is the one who is in a different place from us, a place from which he chooses to come and visit those who love him and from which he may choose to intervene in the workings of the world on our behalf. The world beyond is the site of power and significance – relationships only enter into the spiritual realm when one of the members of the relationship has died and become part of this other world, attaining something of its holy resonance. This transcendent God, who deigns from his goodness to be immanent, is often most easily encountered within the sacred spaces set aside for worship – church buildings. These are places where horizontal relationships may be important and, certainly, help to strengthen an individual's attachment to a particular church, but where the vertical relationship is the crucial one. The women go to church to be nearer to God, not to be nearer to one another. The community there is not just one of the women who go today, but of all the others who have been part of the Church in this world and are still felt to be part of it in the world beyond.

One possible meeting point for these two drastically different maps of the presence of God lies in the area of religious experience. The nature of the experiences the women described was deeply individual and characteristically appeared as encounters with something deeply 'other'. In this they still seem to be far away from feminist ideas about spirituality. However, these were not experiences that demanded change and transformation, they did not rupture existing relationships or call for these to be abandoned in the quest for closer communion with God. They were, rather, experiences of comfort and affirmation within existing circumstances, providing the necessary strength to go on, rather than the impetus to leave. In this, they can be seen to affirm the relationality at the heart of feminist thought and assert that the Christian life can, even should, be lived out amid the commitments of family and community rather than at one remove from the muddle of daily life. God may be at home in a different place, but Christians are to be at home in this world, while receiving help and encouragement from the other.

Any adequate model of the Church will need to take into account the impetus to worship as well as the need to affirm the bonds of community. Letty Russell's round table and kitchen table need to be supplemented with some form of altar table – a place where the transcendence of God is affirmed as well as God's presence in our midst. There seems to be less need among these working-class women for the Church to provide their base experience of human community – they are rooted in one area alongside people who have shared the same experiences of life. Their church is a space where they can step outside the demands of the relationships that bind them to family and community and find a place where they are alone with God. It would be a sad loss to see feminist models of the Church depriving working-class women of this much-needed 'breathing space'. It would also be a sad loss were the feminist insistence on the Church as a community for doing justice to disappear. The question is, how we can build a Church community that meets both needs and does not turn the Church into a middle-class enclave in areas where it has so far escaped that fate.

It may be, as Callum Brown asserts, that the ageing generation of churchgoing women who formed the bulk of my research are the last of a dying breed. However, Brown's deterministic views on why women attend church do not do justice to the depth of spiritual awareness that fuels these women's continued search for God. Feminist, and other, theologians committed to speaking a theology that welcomes the contributions from other women's voices need to take seriously the ways in which these women encounter God. The question of whether or not such disparate voices can find some sort of harmony together is addressed in the final chapter of this book.

Notes

1 *Becoming Divine: Towards a Feminist Philosophy of Religion*, Manchester: Manchester University Press, 1998, p. 269, emphasis as in the original.
2 Sallie McFague, *The Body of God: An Ecological Theology*, London: SCM, 1993, p. 149, emphasis as in the original.
3 *Life Abundant: Rethinking Theology and Economy for a Planet in Peril*, Minneapolis: Fortress, 2001, p. 140.
4 *New Woman, New Earth: Sexist Ideologies and Human Liberation*, 2nd edition, Boston: Beacon, 1995.

5 London: SCM, 1992.

6 *Gaia and God*, p. 1.

7 *Gaia and God*, p. 254.

8 This concept is explored with the whole area of church later in this chapter.

9 She also saw a face with swollen cheeks superimposed on the image and, the next week, suffered dreadful toothache. She sees the vision as God's way of saying he would be with her through the pain.

10 In the words of Liz, from St Aidan's, 'I'm not a great pray-er, I must admit I'm not. I always want to be but I've never cracked praying.'

11 She was also given a prayer card for St Peregrine, the patron saint of those suffering from cancer, and used to light a candle and pray to him each day.

12 Linda Woodhead, 'Feminist theology – out of the ghetto?' in Deborah F. Sawyer and Diane M. Collier (eds), *Is There a Future for Feminist Theology?*, Studies in Theology and Sexuality 4, Sheffield: Sheffield Academic Press, 1999, p. 205.

13 For a fuller picture, see Natalie Watson, *Introducing Feminist Ecclesiology*, London: Continuum, 2002.

14 London: SPCK, 1993.

15 *Wisdom of Fools*, p. 129.

16 See *Prophecy and Mysticism: The Heart of the Postmodern Church*, Edinburgh: T. & T. Clark, 1997, Chapter 1.

17 Louisville, Kentucky: Westminster/John Knox, 1993.

18 *Church in the Round*, p. 25, emphasis as in the original.

19 There are, of course, writers who work in the construction of feminist forms of Christian worship, but the nature of worship itself is a largely unexplored region.

20 Detailed descriptions of each church can be found in Chapter 2.

21 This was Tina, who attends St Justin's only so that her daughter can go to Sunday school and who does not think of herself as a church-going person or a woman of faith.

22 The school Liz refers to is St Aidan's C. of E. Primary School, which is closely attached to St Aidan's Church.

23 The whole question of men's and women's roles in church is discussed later in this chapter.

24 Even the dilapidated St Mark's is not allowed to sink into complete disarray.

25 Both these answers were from members of the evangelical Anglican congregation.

26 Liz, from St Aidan's.

27 Enid, from St Justin's. Enid, like others among the Catholic women, was also in favour of a married priesthood and saw celibacy as an unreasonable burden to place on priests.

28 London and New York: Routledge, 2001.

29 *The Death of Christian Britain*, Introduction, pp. 9–10.

30 Beverley Skeggs makes similar points about the role of women as moral guardians and this role's particular impact on working-class women in *Formations of Class and Gender*, London: Sage, 1997, Chapter 3.

31 *The Death of Christian Britain*, p. 196.

32 Oxford: Blackwell, 1994.

33 *Religion in Britain*, p. 122, emphasis as in the original.

6

'I DIDN'T THINK DEATH COULD BE BEAUTIFUL'

[The afterlife's] such a mystery. It's a shame . . . that it wasn't put forward more clearly so you knew what was going to happen.

Liz's wish that we had a clearer blueprint for what happens when we die is likely to ring a bell with many contemporary Christians. As Bryan Turner comments in the chapter of his book *Religion and Social Theory* in which he examines Christian attitudes to death and sex:

> Belief in life after death, along with the whole mythology of heaven, hell and resurrection, has become an optional extra of modern Christian life.[1]

He comes up with the currently orthodox hypotheses that death has replaced sex as the great unmentionable and that modern life is organised so as to keep its reality as far away from daily experience as possible. Death no longer needs to be explained by religion because it is no longer an accepted part of daily life. Instead, it has been relegated to the status of an embarrassment: 'Death has been routinised as the province of experts and professionals so that death "demands no meaning of a kind which religion has traditionally supplied".[2] It is against this contemporary background that the attitudes of both the East End women and the feminist theologians and philosophers of religion need to be examined.

The issue of death and what, if anything, happens after it, was saved till late on in each interview. This conscious decision on my part reflects the contemporary wariness of raising the subject in conversation and was intended to allow the interviewees the chance to relax into the interview before they were asked to confront what might be emotionally sensitive material. In some cases, this was not the first time that death had been mentioned – it quite frequently came up when the interviewee was describing her life and its most memorable events. The questions about death moved from the general 'What do you think happens when someone dies?', through more detailed enquiries about the interviewees' ideas of heaven, hell and purgatory to a final question of whether or not Christianity would make sense to them if it only dealt with this world. This stage of the interviews was often marked by tears, usually held back, but still expressing the depth of the pain involved. There is no doubt that death was one of the most emotive subjects covered, but none of the women were reluctant to talk about their feelings in this area. A few of them did apologise for the tears that gathered in their eyes, but, in general, there was a sense that this was an area where tears were expected and right and that did not become more painful as a result of being talked about.

Despite the fact that death is, as Bryan Turner points out, typically a professionalised and institutionalised event nowadays, there were several women who had been with their relatives at their death and some of them related experiences to do with the passing out of life. These were, on the whole, positive experiences, although one interviewee spoke of the presence of death in more ambivalent terms. Amy had twice experienced a slightly sinister feeling of a 'doorkeeper or a guard' when viewing dead bodies. This 'death presence' was only there with the dead body until a living person came in. In fact, Amy rang me up after the interview to make sure that I understood this presence properly, telling me that it was 'not an enemy, but just doing its job' – a natural, though frightening, part of life. When Amy spoke of her own mother's death, she described it as a very natural process, with no slightly spooky visitor. However, even in this case, there was a sense of someone else being involved in the dying process. Amy describes her mother saying clearly, 'No, I'm not ready' to someone only she could see and only finally dying when Amy reassured her that it was all right to go.[3]

This sense that the dying person is going into another presence is echoed in two other accounts. In the first, it is the Virgin Mary who accompanies the Christian soul over the threshold of death:

> I was just praying and talking to her – I know she was uncon-
> scious – and I just felt the presence of Our Lady come into the
> room and I thought she must be going to die ... it was so
> strong the sense of Our Lady being there and she just went, like
> that.[4]

Susan was not surprised by the Virgin Mary's presence as she believes this to be one of the promises that are made to those who say the rosary. She described the experience as being accompanied by a sense of 'this tremendous peace' and gave the impression that it was a right and gentle end of life. Enid also spoke of death as peaceful and accompanied by a sensation that the dying person was being welcomed into a new form of life. In this case, it was her mother who died and the welcoming presence was contained in the sound of the church bells ringing at the moment of her death. Enid commented to me about her daughter, 'And even Emma said "Mum, I didn't think death could be beautiful, but that was."'

The souls of the departed share certain characteristics in most of the women's accounts. Their existence is seen as entirely separate from that of the material body that they had inhabited, with a dualistic understanding of matter and spirit. Enid, from St Justin's, put this view very clearly:

> I wouldn't disrespect the body when it's dead, but I've got no
> feelings for it ... When you hear people going to see their dead

– I could never think about doing that because once their spirit's left them to me they're alive still.

The body is just the covering that is put aside when the spirit, the true essence of the person, is set free. This means that it would still be possible to recognise one's loved ones when meeting them again after death. They would no longer look the same as they had on Earth, but something of their essence would still identify them as the person they had once been. Marie, from St Justin's, likened this to the experience the disciples had in both recognising and not recognising Jesus when he returned to them after the resurrection. Amy, from Green Memorial Methodist Church, made the same connection:

> But the knowing of the person wasn't in the features. It was in the heart and the spirit or soul. And it was strangely enough in those actions – the breaking of the bread – that they recognised him. Yeah, I think there'll be a recognition, but it won't be as it is now.

The essence of the self is not in its physical reality but in its spiritual identity, which death fails to interrupt. The physical body breaks down in decay, but the integrity of the self is separate from, and untouched by, this natural process.

It is interesting to follow these personal reflections on death with the insights of sociologists looking at death in the context of society as a whole. Both death and the body have, indeed, recently been the focus of considerable sociological interest, as they provide valuable insights into contemporary understandings of the self. Tony Walter has been at the forefront of this thinking and traced three historical phases in attitudes to death: traditional, modern and neo-modern. The traditional phase is characterised by death being quick and frequent – plague rather than cancer as the archetypal killer, occurring within the context of the community and being both explained and overseen by religion. This medieval pattern gradually gave way to a modern order in which death became a hidden occurrence within a context where private and public competed for precedence and religious authority was replaced by medical know-how. In Walter's opinion, this phase is just now being modified by a neo-modern pattern in which death has become a prolonged event in a context that combines the private and public and in which the ultimate authority is the self – 'I did it my way' being the motto.[5]

These changes to the way in which society typically tackles death have allowed changes in the way society explains death to itself. These changes are part of the very different ways in which the self, and the body as part of the self, is understood. Death, as Chris Shilling points out, has become 'a radically unnatural occurrence' within a culture in which the body is believed to be under the control of the individual.[6] Our body is no longer a given with which we have to come to terms – an entity that has decay and death as part of its normal lifecycle. Instead, it is just the starting point for a 'life-long project' in which our levels of health and physical attractiveness are believed to be the result of our own choices and decay can be both delayed and disguised.

As Shilling notes, treating the body as a life-long project calls for the investment of resources. These resources are partly financial – beauty treatments and gym memberships do not come cheap – and partly social – the capital of education and confidence that facilitate the presentation of an attractive personality in the eyes of the dominant culture. These are resources that are far more readily available to middle-class people than members of the working and under classes who are to be found on the estates of Walker and Byker. It is not surprising, therefore, to find that the worldview of these women is one where worth is still judged and based on moral character rather than personality and looks. The former is an attribute that is more under their control. They may not have the resources to make their body and personality a 'life-long project' that will be rewarded with social appreciation, but they are able to make their own ethical choices. In this way, they are within the established pattern of working-class respectability examined by social theorists from Timothy Jenkins to Beverley Skeggs.[7]

These moral attributes are not necessarily rewarded with success in this life, but, when combined with a religious faith that looks for meaning beyond the self, do provide the traditional underpinning necessary for a 'good death' – 'that is, a death in which the individual retains to the end a sense of the meaningfulness of their body, their self-identity and the social world.'[8] In this worldview, death is not quite the disaster it is for those whose investment has been centred on their own physical well-being. The focus on health and the semblance of youth renders death especially dreadful and makes it a failure as well as an ending.[9] In Tony Walter's opinion, this position is compounded by the failure of the neo-modern view of death to provide a philosophical framework in which to contemplate it: 'Postmodernism is a culture born out of the very success of modernism in controlling nature, and I am yet to be convinced that it has the philosophical resources to enable human beings to come to terms with their ultimate powerlessness.'[10]

The sociology of the body and death makes it clear that the contemporary view of self is ill equipped to deal with the occurrence of death. The emphasis on investing financial and social capital in ensuring our own physical well-being means that the loss of it is the greatest waste that can be imagined. It is only bearable if the individual self can be seen, by themselves and by others, to have reached a reasonable level of fulfilment in this life. Death, the ultimate loss of self-control, is the ultimate postmodern humiliation.

For the women I interviewed, however, death is neither a humiliation nor an end. They showed considerable interest in where these detachable souls go to after death and the possible future fulfilment that might still be open to them. They had a variety of mental pictures of the heavenly realm, which were usually prefaced with disclaimers that these were only imaginative guesses. Mention was made of mansions, light, beautiful music, lovely green fields and gardens of roses. Most people found it easier to believe in heaven than visualise what it might look like or what eternity would feel like, but there were some with clear expectations. These were not focused on the physical environment of the afterlife, but on what would be at the heart of the experience. These expectations can be grouped around three different focus points: continued spiritual growth, union with God and reunion with the beloved dead.

There were those who saw the afterlife as a place where the soul continued to grow closer to God – a place of continued activity rather than mere passive enjoyment. Two of the women spoke of different stages as the soul grew gradually into its full glory. As Marie expressed it, 'I think there'll be different stages even in the next world, you know. Where we'll start off, you know, and you'll climb to different places, higher and higher.' Thus, death does not put a full stop to the person's spiritual development and activity, but allows growth to continue in a new context. This life is seen as being too short to contain all the necessary learning that the human being has to acquire, so this continues within the realm of eternity: 'We'll probably be doing more there than we are here!'

However, more important for most people when considering heaven was its role as the place where families are reunited and relationships severed by death are once again restored:

> That's the way I look at it – building the family group back. Um, because I have a young niece who was only seven when she died and, when Alice died, we said, 'Well, you're taking care of Hannah now.' Grandad's going to look after you – this is the way I perceive it.[11]

Again and again, heaven was spoken of as a place for meeting up with lost relatives and it was this expectation that made the experience of death and loss bearable. Relationships would still define people – they would still be 'mum' or 'grandad' in heaven, even though their appearance, and their ages, might have changed. This reunion was sometimes described as extending to 'angels and saints' or other members of the local community: 'Ada once said,

"If you go first, put a sign up and say Byker people here."' (Jane, from St Mark's).

In most of the interviewees' eyes the community of heaven is a close replica of the community of Earth, but with all that is painful and distressing removed. We continue being the same people there that we have been here, just freed from our earthly restrictions and with our true natures no longer disguised by our bodily appearances.

The only group of women who did not prioritise family reunion in heaven were those interviewed from St Mark's. For this more evangelical cohort, heaven is first and foremost the place where the Christian is united with God. As Catherine said:

> That's the traditional thing – that we're going to meet in heaven
> – but . . . it won't matter because it's going to be – you're going
> to be in God's glory, so whatever else is there won't matter.

Family might be there, but it will be the meeting face to face with God that is heaven's defining feature. In the words of Catherine's sister, Angela, 'He [God] will be revealed, and that's the purpose of life.'

In this view, the soul still retains its separate and particular nature and enters into a new relationship with God, rather than being absorbed into the divine life. This group of women were also the only ones who spoke with any conviction of the existence of hell as a place of punishment. As Angela put it, 'Because if you believe in heaven you've got to believe in hell. Um, because it's there, it's a fact, the devil's there . . . Yes, I believe there's a hell, and I'm working very hard not to get sent there.'

The fear of hell is seen as an important motivation in bringing people to faith and keeping their behaviour ethical when they believe. The women do not categorise very closely who will be condemned to hell, but believe that Christian faith and good behaviour are the only ways that guarantee escape. This causes some of them to fear that they may not meet their loved ones again in heaven, but they trust that this will not be allowed to cause them pain when they are in God's closer presence.

The reactions of women from the other churches to questions about hell were more mixed. Three of them were quite definite in their opinion that it was this world that was hell:

> You see I've said for years . . . this is the way I think – this, this is hell and when you die you go to heaven . . . There must . . . be a better place than this to live in 'cos there's that many drugs and killings and shootings. Paradise, that's where I think you go to, that's beautiful.[12]

Tracy and some of the others could not imagine that God would do anything worse to people than the experiences they had undergone in their own lives or the suffering they had seen in the lives of others. This world was not for them a place of potential and growth, but a prison of low expectations and powerlessness. There was no chance of their finding personal fulfilment or self-realisation within their familial and social setting and they could not believe that this was all that God wanted for them. Their previous experience did not cause them to look for change and improvement within this lifetime, but they could still hope for their potential for joy and transcendence to be realised in the world to come.

Even those others for whom this world was not an unrelieved vale of tears placed little value on traditional teachings about hell. The emphasis was far more strongly on the 'God who wants to make you happy' than on the need for eternal punishment. There was some tension expressed about the need for differentiation between 'normal' people and those who had committed acts of cruelty, but this was resolved – at least for the Roman and Anglo-Catholic interviewees – in the idea of purgatory:

> And I think it [purgatory] is just like a preparation place where you're being purified. You kind of get purified on your journey

here, but you still maybe need it, in different degrees. (Susan, from St Justin's)

There was some tension visible also in the way that the interviewees struggled with answering questions about hell. A number expressed the view that it was something that they didn't like to think about, while others talked of the way in which they had been frightened by the idea as children, but had discarded it as they grew up. For some, even the idea of purgatory was seen to militate too strongly against God's essentially merciful nature: 'I think when you go, you will just be with God. Yeah, I can't really see there being purgatory even – because he forgives all, doesn't he? (Ruby, from St Justin's)

The overall impression was that there was enough suffering in this life without imagining the need for further suffering after death. God was going to make things right for everyone, even though some might need a time for cleansing before they would be fit to come into God's presence.

It will readily be imagined from all of the foregoing that, for the women I interviewed, Christianity is, at its heart, a religion of the 'other world' as much as a religion of this world. When asked whether or not Christianity would still be relevant to them if it only taught about this life, most struggled to make sense of the question. There was only one who wholeheartedly endorsed a Christianity that had its teaching restricted to this world only; for the others it was not only Christianity's *teaching* about the next world that was seen as essential, but the fact that that other world existed. It, rather than any transformation of their current circumstances, was the focus of their greatest hope and of their only expectation of true fulfilment.

The idea of self that lies behind these beliefs about life after death is clearly based on a traditional dualistic understanding of the divide between the soul and the body. The body is a temporary shell that is discarded at death without anything fundamental to the person being lost in this division. The body is not even seen as essential for recognition as spirits will somehow know each other, even though their appearance will have completely altered. It is the soul that carries the identity of the self – an identity that is eternal and radically free from the decay of the material world. The hope is that this eternal essence will find a home waiting in the heavenly realm in which it will continue relationships with family and friends, as well as encountering God and achieving spiritual maturity. There is the possibility that judgement may involve time spent being cleaned of all impurities before being able to enter heaven and, for a minority of the women, there is still a very real fear of being condemned to an eternity of punishment.

This picture of the body–soul relationship is as far as it is possible to be from the contemporary philosophical orthodoxy on the nature of human selfhood. The unwillingness to accept the possibility of identity survival without the survival of body – or at least of the brain – is widespread in the philosophical community. One eminent example is Martha Nussbaum, who finds any accounts of human nature that make claims of bodily transcendence unfeasible and fantastical:

> Her objection is always to the sorts of aspirations to transcending humanity which would deprive us of our humanity – 'we are bodily finite beings of a particular sort, beings who go through time in a particular way' – immersed 'in the characteristic movements of human time and the adventures of human finitude'.[13]

This school of philosophy, which refuses to see possibilities of transcending the body, is criticised by theologian Sarah Coakley. She sees it as limiting the capacity for human potential and trapping contemporary thought within a narcissistic worldview. She describes the current orthodoxy as:

> Devoid now of religious meaning or of the capacity for any fluidity into the divine, shorn of any expectations of new life

beyond the grave, it has shrunk to the limits of individual fleshliness; hence our only hope seems to reside in keeping it alive, youthful, consuming, sexually active and jogging on (literally), for as long as possible.[14]

Not all feminist theologians, or philosophers of religion, react with such negativity to a philosophy that rules out any form of existence apart from the physically embodied. Grace Jantzen makes such a view fundamental to her own thinking. Her attitude to death is, in fact, somewhat ambivalent. She follows Hannah Arendt in wanting to replace the word 'mortal' with the word 'natal' to describe our human nature – changing the focus from the fact that everyone dies to the fact that everyone is born. However, she also wants us to face our profoundly finite nature:

> I suggest that a feminist philosophy of religion must have as one of its highest priorities the root-and-branch eradication of such valorisation of infinity, and its replacement with an acceptance of limits, for ourselves, for the earth, for the divine. Finitude is not evil.[15]

There is real crusading fervour in this language, which suggests how strongly Jantzen feels about the subject. Her motivation seems to be two-fold: both a desire for human beings to accept reality and think through its religious consequences and a conviction that ethical behaviour towards the world and its inhabitants can only be securely rooted in a rejection of all 'escapist' fantasies of other, compensatory, worlds. Wistful musings about infinity only serve to cloud our perceptions of reality and offer an excuse for permitting injustice to continue in the hope that everything will be put right after we die. These must be put aside so that we can concentrate on the serious business of living in this world and attempting to improve the experience for all 'natals'.

The acceptance of Jantzen's reality means replacing 'salvation' as a central religious metaphor with 'flourishing'. This substitution is important to Jantzen as it keeps the divine activity within the borders of the natural world, rather than suggesting that it comes as intervention from an outside realm. There is no 'other place' from which a saviour could come or to which rescued humanity could be transported. Instead, all human well-being has to be located within the natural and social world as we know it here and now. In Jantzen's view, this is the necessary philosophical underpinning of an ethical urgency that will make the achievement of the conditions under which all human beings can flourish its one priority. This would correct the contemporary overemphasis on the individual – both by making the flourishing of all people the central focus and by emphasising that the divine is to be found within the web of human relationship rather than on another, 'higher', plane. Transcendence does not lie in a spiritual way of being that is entered after death, but in our full realisation of our human capacities, particularly our capacities for relationships: 'To have the capacity for transcendence does not entail having the capacity, now or in the future, to become disembodied, but rather to be embodied in loving, thoughtful, and creative ways.'[16]

This denial of traditional Christian understandings of transcendence is at the heart of much feminist theology also. Rosemary Radford Ruether's work *Gaia and God*,[17] epitomises this central strand in Christian feminist theology, which has entirely abandoned belief in an afterlife. Although she wants to retain the idea of transcendence contained within traditional understandings of the word 'God', she does not want to propagate a theology that sees human identity as needing the validation of an eternal dimension. Human life has to be seen entirely within the context of this material word – the 'Gaia' of her title, which is a sacred matrix of relationship. Sacred not in the sense of being inhabited by a divine consciousness, but in the sense of being a site of ultimate value. On death, the human person is reabsorbed within this matrix and, by the physical decay of the body, helps to provide the nourishment for the web of relationships to continue. Human encounter with God takes place entirely in a this-worldly context and ethical endeavour is solely focused on improving this life, rather than aiming for a reward hereafter.[18]

This ecological understanding of the lifecycle – in which natural processes replace divine intention as the deciding factor in both life and death – is common across feminist theology and does not solely belong to its Christian manifestations. Carol Christ's early writings in particular show an entirely this-worldly focus, in which life and death are part of the whole dance of existence and need no other meaning apart from this:

> The divinity that shapes our ends is life, death, and change, understood both literally and as metaphor for our daily lives. We will never understand it all . . . Death may come at any time. Death is never early or late. With regard to life and death there is no ultimate justice, for there is no promise that life will be other than it is . . . Knowledge that we are but a small part of life and death and transformation is the essential religious insight.[19]

This is immanence and finitude taken to their logical conclusion – a place where there is no room left for transcendence, human or divine, except as that which is (mis)interpreted in terms of the achievement of full human potential in relationship.

It is not, of course, just 'my death' that human beings have to come to terms with, but also 'your death' and how I will cope when you are no longer around. Indeed, in the interviews, the women talked much more about their experiences of loss and their hopes for their loved ones, than they did about their own possible fate after death. They, like all of us, need a strategy that allows them to mourn, but not to be debilitated by their loss. It will be seen how this is provided by their current system of belief and whether or not a feminist framework would also be able to facilitate this process.

The deaths spoken of most frequently, and with most feeling, were those of children and mothers. I was asked more than once whether or not my own mother was still alive and advised to both cherish her and expect her death to be devastating. Although fathers' deaths were also referred to, these did not carry the same emotional charge for most of the interviewees and the loss of a father was not seen to mark a turning-point in the same way. I was never asked whether or not my father had died. Those who had lost children obviously found these the hardest deaths to come to terms with, as they seemed to be against the ordinary course of nature. It was these deaths that caused real anger with God and the questioning of faith. Ivy, a long-time member of St Justin's, remembers the time when her daughter's illness and eventual death caused her to avoid the Church:

> And sometimes turning against, I shouldn't say it, but turning against my religion. I shouldn't, 'cos he's [God's] there for everybody regardless, but at the time you don't think rationally.

Enid, also from St Justin's, remembers her anger at the loss of her last baby: 'Because I was bitter about losing my baby. Oh, I thought God had been really cruel to us.' Both these women had come to terms with their loss in ways that reconciled them to their faith, but the process had been neither an easy nor an inevitable one.

In these examples, the dead person was felt to have passed on from this world, but there were other occasions when the women spoke of dead relatives still being present in some way. This presence was sensed rather than seen and was acknowledged to be open to other explanations. As Anna, from St Aidan's, said:

> But it has happened, like odd things, and I feel like, you know, it's my mum. But with that sort of thing you always never know whether you're just trying to console yourself. But I do feel like my mum does help us along.

The presence of dead relatives was perceived in strange smells, objects being mysteriously moved to new positions, the sound of bells ringing by themselves and the sound of laughter. The presence was always described as friendly and gave a comforting impression that the deceased was still in relationship with his or her surviving relatives. Edith, a member of St Aidan's in her eighties, spoke of her own experience:

> But when my mother died, this house went icy cold . . . It was dead, cold and dead, for a whole month. And then something happened . . . no sunshine outside, but the whole place was lit up. And we always said that she was back again and would never leave it.

Those women who mentioned such experiences were all also convinced in the reality of heaven as the destination for (at least most) souls after death. This belief was held uncritically alongside the belief that they were visited by the spirits of their dead. The veil between this world and the next seemed to be seen as permeable, able to be crossed by the beloved deceased as well as God and the saints.[20]

The women coped with death by seeing it as an ending, but not a final division. They are very conscious of the reality of the loss that they have suffered and do not deny the pain that such bereavement continues to cause them, even many years later. However, they are not immobilised by such loss because they are able to see it within a worldview in which bodily existence is not the only form of life. Nor does their continuing sense of the presence of the dead mean that they are trapped within a very early stage of the separation process that forms part of mourning. Tony Walter quotes G. Bennett's assessment of such experiences approvingly:

> Bennett considers awareness of the dead to be related to the family-centredness of her women, many of whom had lost an important relative often years or decades before. For them, living in the presence of the dead is not a 'phase' they go through in

the early stages of bereavement, but more like a final resolution of bereavement.[21]

In a very real way, these women see their family circle as being unbroken, though disrupted, by the event of death.

There has not been a great deal of discussion about the process of mourning within feminist philosophy or theology. What there is seems to rely on the stoic acceptance of the reality of finitude, mitigated perhaps by the understanding that the deceased beloved is now providing sustenance for other beings in the great web of life. Beverley Clack, for example, talks of the cycle of life, death and regeneration as all being part of the nature of the goddess.[22] Carol Christ also enjoins women to accept both the comic and tragic as part of life and 'to rejoice and to weep, to sing and to dance, to tell stories and create rituals in praise of an existence far more complicated, more intricate, more enduring than we are'.[23] Human beings are enjoined by these writers to focus on the general continuation of love and life rather than on the loss of that particular love and the ending of that one life.

There are some among the feminist academic community who do not feel that this answers the depth of the lived experience of bereavement and are looking for other ways to deal with loss within a feminist framework. Harriet A. Harris takes issue with Grace Jantzen's picture of God, partly because, in its immanence and vulnerability, it provides no safe refuge for those who mourn:

> The God 'who changest not' provides comfort not by suffering with us but by being less in flux than we are. Yet this changeless God 'abides' with us through our troubles, and so is best not conceived as immutable either . . . Images of a God not subject to decay may bring comfort when facing death, but Jantzen will not think about death. What might this suggest?[24]

Harris accuses Jantzen of side-stepping the whole issue of death because her religious philosophy does not provide the resources for resolving our fears and hopes in this area. Emphasising our nature as natals rather than mortals, she has dismissed mortality as a problem in favour of remaining solely focused on our flourishing in this life. I would agree with Harris that this leaves Jantzen with few resources to offer when life is not flourishing, apart from the exhortation to work for social change, which does not provide immediate personal comfort, only the prospect of eventual general improvement. This is a hope that may seem as illusory to the powerless many at the margins of society as life after bodily death does to her.

Many of the Roman Catholic women I interviewed mentioned the influence of the catechism in framing their childhood ideas about the afterlife. This teaching was remembered as powerfully frightening and quite clear on the three possible destinations of heaven, hell and purgatory.

The Roman and Anglo-Catholic churches also reinforced the continuity of life between this world and the next in their liturgy and, to a certain extent, in their preaching. The liturgical reinforcement is much less at both Green Memorial Methodist and St Mark's, where the tradition of praying for the dead is less accepted and the role of the communion of saints receives less emphasis. St Mark's, however, with its stress on biblical teaching and orthodoxy, does teach its members that the parables of the afterlife – such as the rich man and Lazarus (Luke 16.19–31) – are to be taken literally. It may be relevant that the only woman interviewed who could readily see value in Christianity without the teaching on life after death was a member of Green Memorial Methodist.

The liturgical references to the afterlife fall into two categories: prayers for the dead and the celebration of the communion of saints. The former form part of the intercessions at every Eucharist at St Aidan's, with the names of deceased members of the congregation being read out on the anniversaries of their deaths. In the Roman Catholic mass, too, the dead are remembered in the intercessions and often in the Eucharistic prayer itself, with the words 'Remember, Lord, those who have died and have gone before us marked with the sign of faith, especially those for whom we now pray, N and N. May these, and all who sleep in Christ, find in your presence light, happiness and peace.'[25] As well as this, in both the Anglican and Roman liturgies, the worshippers are reminded of their fellowship with the 'whole company of heaven' and, at both St Aidan's and St Justin's, the intercession of the Virgin Mary is asked on the congregation's behalf. In both these churches, there is a strong overall sense that the living and the dead are divided by only a narrow gap and that Christians can be at home as much in one realm as the other.

This is not to say that all the ministers of the churches[26] do not work hard to ensure that their congregations are aware of this-worldly, as much as other-worldly, concerns. All three current incumbents are committed to working to improve the social welfare of the local inhabitants, whether members of their congregation or not, and promote projects for refugees, young single mothers and community involvement, among many others. However, there is some reluctance on the part of members of their congregations to see such work as a necessary part of their Christian discipleship. The previous vicar of St Aidan's was felt by his congregation to be too interested in pushing a 'political' gospel and not sufficiently focused on spiritual affairs. The message sent out from the pulpits is that God's kingdom is to be sought here and not just in the hereafter, but this does not always convince those who listen to the sermons.

When members of the congregations themselves die, their funerals are usually noticeably different from those of their more secular neighbours. There will normally be a service in church, as well as at the crematorium or grave-side, and in St Justin's and St Aidan's this will usually be a requiem mass. The emphasis in the service is two-fold – both on the sense of bereavement and loss caused by the death and on the hope for eternal life, which means that the loss is not total. Death is seen to be a stage on the human journey rather than the end of it, with God's love holding the person both before and after. This reassuring teaching meant that some of the interviewees felt that they could face death, though not necessarily the dying process itself, without fear. Indeed, one interviewee defined a true Christian (an accolade that she did not feel she was yet able to claim for herself) in the following terms: 'Somebody who absolutely and totally believes in God, and knows that at the end of it they'll go to heaven with Jesus. They're not frightened of dying.'[27]

It seems a natural progression to move on from the Church to considering the communion of saints. In particular, I want to look at Elizabeth A. Johnson's book, *Friends of God and Prophets: A Feminist Theological Reading of the Communion of Saints.*[28] Johnson stands out as a feminist who keeps a commitment to the traditional Christian teaching of life after death and, in particular, the continuing relationship of the Church on both sides of the divide of death. In taking this view, she acknowledges that she stands with a minority in our contemporary society: 'In truth, people in this culture tend to sense as a rule that those who have died have truly disappeared from this world. They are no longer accessible to the living in any direct fashion, as was possible to imagine in a previous age.'[29] However, as has already been seen, the women interviewed did often feel that their dead were still present to them and valued the intermediary abilities of the holy dead (at least in St Justin's and St Aidan's). Johnson might not approve of all the forms in which the women feel that their dead are present to them, while agreeing that their presence is still a truthful possibility. In her final chapter, 'Companions in hope', she argues against *easy* communication with the dead, as they are beyond our imagining and exist in a completely different mode of being, but does not rule out all such communication as impossible.

Johnson wants both to keep and yet redefine the doctrines of heaven, hell and purgatory. In a similar fashion to some of the women interviewed, she sees heaven as a place of vitality rather than static perfection and, again as do some of the interviewees, sees hell as either being empty or self-chosen annihilation. Purgatory in her view is the immediate purging of the evil consequences of our actions. There is no eternal punishment waiting after death, only the possibility of nothingness or of continuing growth in a dynamic afterlife. Marie, a member of St Justin's, has very much the same idea:

> So it's going to be all exciting with different things. And I think there'll always be plenty to do. You know some people think it will just be sitting around in heaven with harps and things like that, but I say you'll get a surprise! We'll probably be doing more there than we are here.

In Johnson then, for the first time, is a feminist theologian whose theology of death does not look out of place when placed next to the hopes and imaginings of the working-class women of the North East. In her chapter 'The darkness of death', having stated that she finds Ruether's 'recycling scenario' both brave and ethically valuable, she goes on to say:

> While I agree that patriarchal eschatology undoubtedly overemphasizes transcendence in a dualistic way that links hope with otherworldliness and disparages female bodiliness and care for the earth, and while I applaud Ruether's emphasis on the importance of ecological consciousness for a living planet, I suggest that a solely immanentist end is not the only conceivable possibility, even within an ecological and feminist perspective.[30]

In other words, Johnson wants a theology that values this world and cares for its needs and the needs of all human people, but she does not see that such a theology would necessarily remove all possibility of an afterlife. In her opinion, it is still theologically and philosophically possible to hold such concerns together with a hope that death is not the final end of human individuals.

Indeed, Johnson's interest in sustaining belief in life after death is not just theological but also grounded in ethical issues of agency and justice. Against Ruether's insistence that ethical action requires an entirely immanentist perspective, she argues that:

> the experience especially of poor women articulated in Third World feminist liberation theologies suggests that hope for life with God after death for human persons and the whole Earth not only does not cut the nerve for action on behalf of justice but actually sustains it, especially in violent situations.[31]

Belief in life after death is not an escape mechanism, but a coping mechanism, which both highlights the injustice of the current situation by providing a paradigm of redeemed relationship and provides the courage to address injustice. This courage lies in knowing that, whatever the humiliation or physical hardship encountered in this life, there is still the possibility of fulfilment – both for the individual self and the whole of creation. These are important issues that will continue to be addressed in the next section, looking at other ethnographic work around this area, and in the conclusion.

John Burdick's ethnographic work in Brazil was intended to answer some very specific questions about the limitations on the success of Roman Catholic base communities, known as CEBs (short for *communidad(e) eclesial de base*). In particular, Burdick wanted to assess their attractiveness to the poor in comparison with the other religious options of *umbanda* – the indigenous Brazilian folk religion based on mediums being possessed by spirits – and the Pentecostal churches, adherents of which are known as *crentes*, believers. His study – described in his book, *Looking for God in Brazil: The Progressive Catholic Church in Urban Brazil's Religious Arena*[32] – was conducted at the end of the 1980s and concentrated on the town of São Jorge in one of the suburbs of Rio de Janeiro. Burdick examined the religious arena in this town in order to answer his central question: 'Why are the CEBs losing the battle for souls? What do Pentecostalism and *umbanda* signify and offer to Brazil's masses that the People's Church does not?'[33]

The answer, not surprisingly, is multifaceted. One of the key factors he identifies is that the CEBs stress the connections between the secular and religious identities of their members, whereas in Pentecostal churches, the emphasis is on the rupture between the convert's previous identity in the world and their new identity as a believer. These theological differences result in the formation of very different groups. The Roman Catholic communities tend to mirror the class distinctions of the wider society and do little to prevent the continuation of power relationships and personal grudges between individual members. The Pentecostals, on the other hand, expect their church to be a distinct community in which authority relies on openness to the Holy Spirit rather than on a secular role or skills such as literacy.

The 'this-worldly' and 'other-worldly' aspects of the two churches seem to lie at the heart of their appeal or lack of it. Strictures on the material and political emphasis of the CEBs were often made by the Catholics who had not subscribed to the new teaching coming from the radical priests. They also even come from those who were attempting to participate in the new organisations:

> The liberation of the world is going to be by grace, it will not depend on our movements ... Look, John, Christ came to struggle for heaven, not for the earth. He came to do the will of the Lord, not to give us material things. Wouldn't you rather have eternal salvation than a piece of bread?[34]

Christianity is still seen as a religion the main focus of which is hope in the hereafter and so a theology that downplays this aspect of the faith is considered by many of the Brazilian poor to be short-changing them. The appeal of the Pentecostals is that this focus is retained at the centre of their worship and belief – a fact recognised by some Brazilian liberation theologians themselves:

> I think that we, without realising it, secularised ourselves more than we thought. We secularised ourselves in our liturgies,

emptying them of the sacred; we secularised ourselves in a mass of debates ... they end up doing ideology and not celebrating God. And then they complain that people are going to other sects, where they sing to God. We don't know how to sing to God. We don't know how to live a profound spirituality.[35]

Burdick concludes from his study that, despite the local and temporary successes of the CEBs, they cause resentment and alienate potential members due to their 'overemphasis on material welfare, to the neglect of eternal salvation'.[36] Their stress on human responsibility for transforming the present world, he goes on to say, 'appears to have rather limited religious appeal'.[37] The poor of Brazil – like the working-class women in my interviews – seem to want their religion to offer them more than a strategy for improving their present circumstances, although they may value this as an adjunct to the central message. Having a clear message of life after death does not necessarily turn their interest away from this world, but, rather, strengthens their ability to cope with the harsher circumstances of their lives and offers the clearer possibility of transformation. I want to finish this section, and lead into the conclusion, with a quote from Burdick that sums up the need to listen to the voices of those facing marginalisation rather than decide, paternalistically or maternalistically, what their needs are:

We would do better to realise that every gesture of resistance carries a seed of reinforcement, every act of reinforcement a seed of resistance. When we do, we remember the importance of discovering how others themselves talk, feel and think about the relationship between what they do and how they experience domination. And when we remember that, we will stop expecting others to fit into our, rather than their, vision of the world.[38]

It has become glaringly obvious in the course of this chapter that the views on death and eternity of many feminist philosophers and the eco-feminist theologians are miles away from those of the women with whom I spoke. The reasons for this may not lie in the academics' greater philosophical and theological sophistication – although they are doubtless able to express their views in more academically respectable language – but in the different life (and death) experiences that ground their own particular standpoints. It is my argument that these different kinds of theology, and the spirituality to which they contribute, answer the very different needs that these different groups experience.

The women I interviewed had frequently had close experiences with the physical actuality of death, as well as with its emotional impact. They talked about death quite easily, knowing it as a reality that has to be faced rather than avoided. This talk was often not without tears as the pain of life without beloved members of the family – most especially, mothers and children – was still very apparent to them. However, they were, without exception, confident that those they had lost physically were still, in some sense, living. For most of the women, this meant that they were either with God or on their way – either in heaven or in purgatory. For a few, it meant that they had faced judgement and would be receiving either eternal reward or eternal punishment. In either case, the self – the core that made that person recognisable as an irreplaceable individual – was not identified with the body, but with the soul – a soul that would still be recognisable, but in a new and different form.

These women do not seem to fit easily within any of the sociological categories of death described by Tony Walters. Death is not the quick and communal event for them that it was in the medieval period, but neither is it the hidden occurrence in which medical authority has displaced religious,[39] nor do they attempt an 'I did it my way' ideal. Instead, they reveal an openness to the reality of death, experienced within the private sphere, in which religious hope continues to have a central role. This also means that they do not view death as the ultimate loss of self-control, carrying with it the entire end of the self and the loss of all personal capital.

The body project has not displaced the soul project for the women I interviewed.

Their beliefs were reinforced by the way in which death was talked of in the churches, providing a strong sense of the continuity of the Christian community across the divide of physical death. Although many of the women had moved away from the traditional teaching of judgement and hell, they had kept the Christian virtue of hope focused on the possibilites that lay beyond the grave. It is the focus of this hope that is criticised by much feminist philosophy and theology. Their argument is that such a focus prevents sufficient attention and energy being put into changing things for the better in this world and dupes its adherents into accepting less than they should in this life. They put forward in its place an immanent view of divinity in which all life is held within the boundaries of the natural world and death is a complete end of the individual, which, in the processes of recycling, allows the web of life as a whole to continue. This view is appropriately expressed in Beverley Clack's quotation from Dylan Thomas: 'Though lovers be lost love shall not/And death shall have no dominion.'[40] Death has no dominion because life continues even when individual lives do not. This theology goes hand in hand with a movement within Western society to identify the self with the body and self-worth with youth and health. Hope for fulfilment in both these cases rests in this lifetime alone and separation at death is final.

It appears to me that such a theology, as with such a lifestyle, centred on achievement within this lifespan, would be profoundly debilitating for the working-class women in these four churches. It would remove from them their hope for themselves and for their loved ones. As we have seen, their life circumstances do not offer either the opportunities for making their body into a life-long project or of achieving the fulfilment they would wish for in other areas of their lives. As John Burdick found in his work in Brazil, it is a religion that includes the possibility of transcending the present world that offers the best survival strategy – and possibility of flourishing – to women and men in deprived circumstances.

They may not have control over the daily circumstances of their lives, but they do have some degree of control over their final, eternal destination – a destination that offers them a validation not proffered by their society.

This belief in a life after death is not a mere tranquilliser, making the women content with daily deprivation in the hope that all will be made better after death. It has a far more positive effect than this. Knowing that they have an eternal destination after death and an eternal dimension to their self in this life, gives them a sense of self-worth that provides a basis for action and a foundation for self-determination. This is combined with a sense of community that extends to previous generations and gives them an awareness of their place in time as well as space. Without this eternal dimension, it would be all too easy for these women to look at themselves with the eyes of contemporary society and judge themselves, and their families, to be failures. Life after death enables them to live this life with greater courage and confidence rather than it being an unnecessary distraction. It prevents grief from being debilitating, too, and is a source of hope when there is little support for optimism elsewhere.

In Elizabeth Johnson's community of saints, there is room for the women of the East End of Newcastle, whereas in Grace Jantzen's philosophy of natals, and Rosemary Radford Ruether's eco-vision, they seem to be squeezed out. A theology of finitude only offers hope for those who have sufficient power in this life to see the possibility of achievement and fulfilment. The traditional Christian teaching empowers those who find in it a source of self-affirmation and of enlivening hope that they cannot attain otherwise in their lives. To lose it would impoverish and impede flourishing for the women interviewed, which no feminist writer would want to see happen. Eternity still has much to give as a theological resource for many women in the twenty-first century.

Notes

1 Bryan Turner, *Religion and Social Theory*, 2nd edition, London: Sage, 1991 (1983), p. 235. Turner bases what he says here on surveys of American churchgoers that show less than half the laity believe in life after death.

2 *Religion and Social Theory*, p. 235, quoting B. Wilson, *Religion in Secular Society: A Sociological Comment*, London: Watts, 1966, p. 71.

3 Amy is a member of Green Memorial Methodist Church, in her forties.

4 Susan, the convenor of the rosary group at St Justin's, describing the death of her friend's mother.

5 For a much more finely nuanced discussion of this development, see Tony Walter, *The Revival of Death*, London: Routledge, 1994, Chapter 4.

6 *The Body and Social Theory*, London: Sage, 1993, p. 192. Part of an interesting discussion of the body, self-identity and death in Chapter 8.

7 See Timothy Jenkins, *Religion in English Everyday Life: An Ethnographic Approach*, New York: Berghahn, 1999, and Beverley Skeggs, *Formations of Class and Gender*, London: Sage, 1997.

8 *The Body and Social Theory*, p. 179.

9 It is interesting in relation to this point to consider how often death is described in contemporary death notices as a battle that has been lost. The implication seems to be that it is a battle that might have been won rather than death being an inevitability that has to be faced sooner or later.

10 *The Revival of Death*, p. 199.

11 Ivy, from St Justin's. Alice was her daughter, who died in her twenties.

12 Tracy, a mother in her forties from St Justin's. One of Tracy's sons was stealing to support his drug habit and another had attempted suicide.

13 Fergus Kerr, *Immortal Longings: Versions of Transcending Humanity*, London: SPCK, 1997, p. 21, quoting from Nussbaum's *Love's Knowledge: Essays on Philosophy and Literature*, Oxford: Oxford University Press, 1990, p. 391.

14 'The eschatological body: gender, transformation and God', *Modern Theology*, **16**, 1, January 2000, pp. 61–73, 62.

15 *Becoming Divine: Towards a Feminist Philosophy of Religion*, Manchester: Manchester University Press, 1998, p. 155.

16 *Becoming Divine*, p. 271.

17 London: SCM, 1993.

18 Her perspective is summarised in her more recent book, *Women and Redemption* (London: SCM, 1998), in which she says of the redemption of this life that 'it is possible only when we put aside the impossible redemptions of final conquest of limits in a realm of immortal life untouched by sorrow, vulnerability, and finitude', p. 254.

19 'Rethinking theology and nature', in J. Plaskow and C. P. Christ (eds), *Weaving the Visions: New Patterns in Feminist Spirituality*, San Francisco: Harper & Row, 1989, p. 321.

20 It has already been seen in Chapter 5 that, for many of the women interviewed, the true home of God is in the supernatural realm, which is characterised by eternity and will only be entered by human beings at their death.

21 *The Revival of Death*, p. 117, based on Bennett's work *Traditions of Belief: Women, Folklore and Supernature Today*, London: Penguin, 1987.

22 'Revisioning death: a thealogical approach to the "evils" of mortality', *Feminist Theology*, 22, September 1999, pp. 67–77.

23 'Rethinking nature and theology' in Plaskow and Christ (eds), *Weaving the Visions*.

24 'Divergent beginnings in feminist philosophy of religion', *Feminist Theology*, 23, January 2000, pp. 105–18.

25 Quoted from the new edition of *The Sunday Missal*, London: CollinsLiturgical, 1984, Eucharistic Prayer 1.

26 This means the priests at St Justin's and St Aidan's and the minister at Green Memorial Methodist, St Mark's being without an incumbent.

27 Liz, a young (in her late forties) grandmother from St Aidan's.

28 London: SCM, 1998.

29 *Friends of God and Prophets*, p. 19.

30 *Friends of God and Prophets*, p. 197.

31 *Friends of God and Prophets*, p. 197, later in the same paragraph as the previous quotation.

32 Berkeley: University of California Press, 1993.

33 *Looking for God*, p. 5.

34 The comment of a Roman Catholic woman who had been involved in her neighbourhood association for the past three years. Quoted on p. 191 of *Looking for God*.

35 Luiz A. G. de Souza, quoted on p. 229 of *Looking for God*, from his article 'É bom que haja crise', *Vermelho e branco*, 26 March 1992.

36 From the Conclusion of *Looking for God*, p. 225.

37 *Looking for God*, p. 226.

38 *Looking for God*, final paragraph, p. 230.

39 It is interesting to note in this context that the parish priest of St Aidan's, also my husband, is called out to give last rites far more frequently than has happened before to either of us in any of the other parishes where we have served.

40 As quoted in her article cited in note 22.

7

THEOLOGY FROM
THE HEART

The process of researching this book was a fascinating and some-times frustrating one. There was the time when, at the end of a moving and thoughtful interview, I found that the tape recorder had entirely failed to record. There was also the regret that I was not able to persuade more of the members of the Methodist church to join in with the process. However, the delights far outweighed the disappointments. Most delightful of all was the chance to listen to women talk with honesty and passion about their life-long encounter with the living God. They would often begin an inter-view with some trepidation, saying that they would get the answers wrong or they didn't know much about their faith, but, at the end, having listened to themselves, they would feel a renewed sense of confidence – more than one woman commented, 'I didn't realise I knew so much.'

So this final chapter is built on the stories and insights shared in those interviews and uses the material to begin to construct a new theological viewpoint for the Church. It also has foundations within feminist theology because it consciously values the experi-ence of women and is committed to their flourishing. However, what is new is its engagement with the spiritual experience of faithful churchgoing, working-class women – women who do not fit within the feminist fold nor register on the radar of the vast majority of academic theologians. The hope is that this engagement will provide the Church with a rich and grounded theology, a theology that takes seriously the spiritual experiences of members of the community of the Body of Christ whose contribution to the life of this body has been consistently undervalued and, indeed, unheard.

Feminist theology teaches us that it is essential to move away from male images of God if spirituality, including Christian spirituality, is going to be a source of strength rather than weakness for women. A male God is too closely connected with patriarchal patterns of power and control to be comfortable and, even were a male God who subverts patriarchy to be envisaged, it would still not help women to see themselves as made in the divine image. Two of the most interesting alternatives come from philosophers of religion Luce Irigaray and Grace Jantzen, with their reimagining of a divine genealogy and a divine horizon. God becomes imagined in terms of the mother–daughter rather than father–son relationship and is also, especially by Jantzen, brought down to Earth to provide a goal, or maybe template, for human becoming in this world.

Against this vision of a spirituality that would allow women to flourish must be set the reality of spiritual understanding for working-class, churchgoing women for whom feminism is an alien concept. Here we have discovered a spirituality that, while formally avowing the gender neutrality of God, in practice paints God as male and finds the use of female language for God unacceptable. Yet this is seen by the women themselves as in no way disadvantageous. Indeed, the relationship with a male God provides them with much in the way of self-affirmation and strength. There is a strong (hetero) sexualised bond between the women and God, or Jesus, which is as important to them as the concept of fatherly control and care. Motherhood, which has been seen to be such an important concept in these women's lives, forms part of the divine relationship in the person of Mary, the Heavenly Mother and understanding fellow sufferer of motherhood.

On one level, this spirituality could be seen as purely destructive. It reinforces the power positions of men and women, with the male only having sufficient gravitas to represent divinity. It can also be seen to serve as a panacea, producing tolerance of an intolerable lot and, therefore, working to prevent transformative change. Women are consoled for their unsatisfactory romantic relationships and for their lack of social power by having an intense relationship with God as the 'perfect male', whose presence in their lives compensates for all other lacks. However, it is also possible to see this spirituality as nurturing a sense of self-worth and providing a necessary survival strategy. The only way in which these women know themselves to be special and of infinite value is by means of their relationship with this divine male. In this relationship they step outside their roles of wife, mother, grandmother, aunt, daughter and are allowed to be Marie or Tracy or Anna and know that their identity is intrinsically lovable. They do not see this relationship as detrimental but as essential to their well-being: it is this that enables them to get through each day.

I would want to affirm that God needs to reflect female as well as male reality. God needs to provide an image for women, an image to which they can aspire and in which they can see themselves valorised and divinised. In other words, they need to see that they reflect the image of God as clearly and fully as men do. Such an image offers the best route for transformation as it speaks of the potential of female fulfilment and sanctification. However, this may not be the aspect of divinity most needed by the women of the St Anthony's estate. For them, God needs to embody power, so that he can help them in their powerlessness, and an unquestioning love, to enable them to face the day knowing that they are not alone. This love is seen through the heterosexual matrix that informs their other relationships, with the romantic love received via Jesus being supplemented by the maternal love received from Mary. This is not a God of transformation, but a God of survival – a God whose chief purpose is to support the individual with a love that only asks love in return.

So what are the implications for a theology of the Church if we take both these spiritual experiences and the insights of feminist theology seriously? I believe that the place we need to start is with the apophatic tradition within Christianity, especially with its central insight that no human language or imagery is sufficient to express the reality of the divine. Just as feminist theologians have had to remind mainstream Christianity that taking Father imagery of God literally is idolatry, so we need to remember that feminist images of God are also limited and fail to express the fullness of the divine reality. This can either drive us to fly from words altogether, as many of the mystics did, or embrace a plethora of images – each partial in itself, but together providing a hint of the spectrum of God's being. This is at the heart of what I have called 'choral theology' – the multiplication of voices singing the Christian story in ways that are true to their particular experience of the Godhead.

Although Grace Jantzen's work has come in for some criticism in this book, I want to rescue one of her key concepts and put it to theological use in this context. Jantzen talks about the importance of doing philosophy of religion with efficacy (efficacy being seen as that which best enables the flourishing of all life within this world) rather than truth as the goal of the endeavour. Jantzen's conclusions about the sort of divine image that would enable such flourishing may be very different from my own, but I agree with her that the concept of flourishing is an important one in itself.

Jantzen's divine is entirely immanent, totally circumscribed by this world, embracing finitude and uniting all being in an interplay of mutual reliance and concern. Whether or not such a divinity has real being is not, for her, the point – the point is that this image of God will best enable humanity to flourish here and now. This divinity, abstract and practically powerless, may perhaps encourage the flourishing of women and men who have a sense of their own ability to shape their lives and are able to wield some amount of power. It will not enable the flourishing of women or men who do not share these privileges.

The God of the women in this study is the God they need – the God who best enables them to flourish in their current circumstances. Their images of a strong male God are efficacious for them in a way that they have long ceased to be for most feminist theologians. This God offers affirmation, a connection to a source of power, constant parental care and also gives some of the women the intensity and fun of romance. The women react to this God with passion, sometimes with anger when he is perceived to have let them down, often with love and trust, occasionally with humour or with fear. In other words, this God is intensely personal with a unique relationship with each woman. This relationship does not enable them to be transformed, but it does enable them to survive, and to survive with hope rather than despair.

This passionate God resonates very deeply with the God of many of the female medieval mystics – the God who embraces them as a husband and delights in his turn in the love that they offer him. Like these medieval women, the relationship is a source of value and purpose, a privilege allowed them by their gender to be the 'Bride of Christ' more fully than any masculine soul could imagine. Theirs is a spirituality deeply rooted in desire – a bodily reaction to God rather than an intellectual one. There is resonance here with contemporary calls for passion and feeling to be allowed to speak theology as well as reason and intellect. The women of St Anthony's estate are not waiting for academic permission to understand their faith in this way, they are doing it quite naturally for themselves.

Unlike Jantzen, I find it impossible to put aside all issues of truth and allow efficacy to have sole sway. However, truth is not, I firmly believe, univocal – it does not speak through one voice alone. This does not mean that there is more than one truth, but that this one truth is not accessible in our limited human condition. In order to get as close to the truth as we can, we need to listen to a multitude of voices, none of which speaks the complete truth but all of which contain some snatches of the truth. This is in the Christian tradition of kataphatic theology, in which God is given a multitude of names as no one word or image can capture the divine plenitude. All of us are limited by the circumstances and experiences of our own lives – none of us can accurately claim a God's-eye view of reality, particularly not of the reality of God.

What prevents a slide into total relativity, where truth is drowned out by a babble of conflicting claims, is the revelation of God's nature in the face of Christ, against which all our portraits of God must be measured.

The transcendent, yet deeply intimate, God who appeared in the words of the women interviewed has a greater reality for me than the pantheistic God who appears in the writings of Jantzen. It is closer to the portrait of Christ as I understand it from the Bible, Christian tradition and my own experience. It is also much closer to the understanding of God that informs orthodox Christianity. However, divine plenitude, divine generosity, means that there is space for both images to be explored and both, I believe, have something to teach us about the ungraspable reality that is God. The important continuing task for Christian theology – feminist and non-feminist – is to show a similar generosity in making room for images of God very different from our own, though still arising out of the Christian tradition. Rather than fearing that we will end up with a jumble of unrelated fragments, we can hope to create a choral theology in which each distinct voice adds to the harmony of the whole. The song needs to be about the flourishing of all God's creation, though the words may need to be translated into languages dictated by particular circumstances.

The focus now moves from looking at how the women define God and relate to the divine to how they see themselves and relate to the people, and the world, around them. Forming the backdrop to this examination is the contemporary emphasis on relationality and its centrality to most feminist, and many ecologically based, spiritualities. What can the way these women live their relationships tell us about their theology of the self in relation to the divine? Does it resemble the feminist conclusions about the place of relationship in life, both material and spiritual? In answering these questions it is hoped that some substance may be added to the very generalised concept of relationality that is of benefit to theology as a whole.

Life is relationship for most of the women interviewed in a

way that it has perhaps ceased to be for the majority of younger middle-class women in Britain today. When the St Anthony's estate women talk about the significant points in their lives, they talk about family and when they speak with most passion, it is about children or parents, especially mothers. They are deeply embedded not only in their own family but also in the larger community: despite the fact that they no longer know all their neighbours, they still know many of them and feel reluctant to move outside the area. Relationships are not uniformly positive – being the greatest cause of sorrow as well as fulfilment and joy – but they are inescapable, having duties attached that it would be somehow unnatural to ignore.

The self-understanding of these women is not founded on individualism and personal achievement, but on their place within an interlocking network of relationships – as daughter, mother, aunt, sister, grandmother, wife, neighbour. This relationality extends to strangers when they enter the community, but hardly to those who remain outside. It most definitely does not extend to the natural world. The web of being, beloved of eco-feminists, means little to those who, like American womanists, feel that they can all too easily be dismissed as bestial by the mainstream culture of their country. It is, for example, a far greater local insult to be called a 'cow' than to be called a 'f***ing' anything else. Relationships in this context mean relationships with others that you have real contact with, not with others who you have never met – it is embodied, and often embattled, real rather than idealistic.

In some ways, this ties in very closely with feminist theories about the self as relational, but it is still a very different way of seeing relationship. These are not freely chosen relationships, they are not a recognition of kinship with the human family and the non-human lives sharing our planet with us, but a concrete set of ties and obligations to particular individuals. In many ways, this is the relationality that some feminists are keen to see change as it defines a woman by those around her rather than by herself. However, before deciding to see it as an evil to be eradicated, or at least severely modified, it is worth pausing to find out if it offers unexpected possibilities for theological and spiritual thinking.

One of the main problems with the image of God discovered in the interviews was that, in its exclusive masculinity, it offered little possibility for the women to see themselves in it. The attributes of God were those of the powerful male, though with an accompanying gentleness, especially in the figure of Jesus, which turned him into the perfect romantic partner. This seemingly offered no image of divinity towards which the women could realistically aspire or by which they could feel their own being vindicated and valorised. God is distant from the women not only because of the gap they perceive between this world and the heavenly realm, of which more later, but also because their gender identities are opposed.

However, this is not the whole story. God is not only characterised as male, but also as *being in relationship*. It has already been seen that God is deeply personal in the iconography of these women's prayer and faith lives; God is known in the relationship that they have with him. Like the women, God has to listen when one of his family wants to talk to him, whether it is to play love records to him or express anger and confusion at the death of a child. God is quintessentially the one who cares, with parental and spousal love, and, therefore, is the one who is in relationship and must be known in the form of relationship. This relationality is as central to the nature of God for these women as his maleness and it is in this relationality that they can see themselves bearing the image of God. They, too, are at the centre of a web of relationships in which demands are made on their attention and goodwill, they too define themselves as people who meet other people's needs and show love to those close to them. Their gender remains different, but their experience of being reflects a relationality that they see at the heart of the Godhead.

This relationality is not limited to God's interaction with humanity, but is present in the internal reality of God as well. God is experienced by most of these women in Trinitarian form, although it must be said that the Spirit comes a poor third to the Father and the Son, with his place occasionally being taken over by 'Our Lady'. However, there is no doubt that relationship is right at the centre of who God is. The picture that comes across is one of family: the more accessible Son leading us to the more remote Father, with the mother providing a third caring presence for the Catholic women. Relationality is integral to the Trinitarian God and this aspect of Godhead finds fuller embodiment in the lives of women – or at least in their own understanding of their lives – than in the lives of men.

This image of a relational God is very different from the panentheistic God we met in Chapter 4 – a God whose body, as Sallie McFague puts it, is the world – but it does point to the same truth about the relational nature of both divinity and humanity. It is the character of that relationship that remains different. In the life experience of the working-class women, relationships are based on interpersonal contact rather than a generalised understanding of the interconnectedness of all life. It is the same with their understanding of relationality and God – it is an interpersonal relationality that is both emotional and committed. This provides affirmation of their own roles within their families and community, though it is questionable in feminist terms whether or not this is a role that we would want to see reinforced. However, as it is the role open to these women and one that they value highly, it can certainly be seen as a positive divine image for survival, though, again, not for transformation. It does have the advantage of looking beyond the I–Thou relationship between the individual and the divine, to the matrix of relationships within the human community and within the Godhead.

The research has, to an extent, vindicated the emphasis within feminist theology and spirituality on the importance of relationality. However, it has also served to highlight the occasionally anaemic and abstract way that relationship is spoken of in feminist writings. Relationality is not always a positive – it can involve unequal demands and the sacrifice of one's own legitimate interests in favour of appeasing others. For many, if not most, women, their relationships are not freely chosen, but involve roles that are laid down by the wider society, including a mixture of opportunities for recognition and fulfilment along with areas where individuality and potentiality are suppressed. However, these relationships, despite their limiting features, help provide a way in to the *imago Dei* when God is also imagined in relational terms. It seems that there is scope here for enfleshing the relationality of feminist spirituality with the bodily encounter that means relationships in the life-world of the women interviewed. A theology that recognises the messiness of human relationships as well as their infinite value comes closest to a genuine theology of incarnation.

By now it will have become apparent that questions of transcendence and immanence are at the heart of much contemporary theology and philosophy, especially that which has been affected by feminist thought. A view of God as transcendent and totally other has traditionally been opposed by feminists, because of its implied disregard for the health and flourishing of this world in favour of escape to a 'better' one. Locating God in a distant heaven is believed to undervalue earthly existence and remove the impetus for social change – that suffering in this life is unimportant as long as the 'other life' awaits in which everything will be put right. In order to correct this, theology needs to locate God within the boundaries of this world. God is either completely contained by the world – as in the pantheism posited by Grace Jantzen – or inhabits the world while also transcending it – as in the panentheism suggested by both Rosemary Radford Ruether and Sallie McFague. In both these formulations, God is primarily to be encountered in our relationships with one another and the interplay of life that animates the material world – finite though it may be.

In contrast, the encounters with God recounted in the interviewing process were more direct. The women did not leave this world, did not enter some 'out-of-body' state in order to meet God, but they did meet him as a visitor to this world rather than as an integral part of it. God is still seen as having some control over the natural ordering of the world, being able to interfere to work for the good of those who ask him in faith. God breaks in to the natural world rather than being contained within it – God is transcendent, yet allows his presence to be felt from time to time. This is not a God whose prime imperative is seen as ensuring human flourishing by means of social change, but, rather, ensuring the individual's flourishing via personal encounter and assurance.

These different takes on transcendence and immanence can be seen as variations in emphasis rather than completely opposite views. God is, in both scenarios, involved with the world – the difference lies in the extent of God's ability to exist and act outside the boundaries of the physical universe. Jantzen is obviously at one end of the spectrum, with the women who see God's 'home' in heaven at the other. In between fall most contemporary Christian theologians and most of the women interviewed. For them, God is encountered here, but not fully known here. It is possible to have a relationship with God, but it is also necessary to hold in mind that God is not contained within our relationships or even within the whole spectrum of relationship that constitutes the web of life. There is something of God that is beyond the natural world, even though there is much of God within it.

It is possible to picture this immanent and transcendent God using the traditional Christian imagery of the Trinity. The first person of the Trinity, the source of all life, is that of the divine which remains outside the created order – the transcendent and ultimate referent of all human striving towards flourishing. This is the divine that remains more than our understanding, beyond our language and outside our emotional grasp. God is encountered within the world via both the second and third persons of the Trinity: God as companion and God as the breath of life. It seems that it is here where the difference lies between the feminist theologians and the women of St Anthony's estate. The immanent God is known to eco-theological thinkers as the pulse of life that animates the universe – the movement and change that character-ises living matter and the interrelationship between different forms of life that allows each to develop and flourish. This is God within, encountered in all other living creatures and life forms and within the matrix of all relationships. However, the immanent God is known differently in the experience of the women in the interviews. For them, God is immanent as a personal presence, a companion and guide to whom they can confide their deepest fears and joys and who will support them in their daily chores and choices. They encounter God in the second person of the Trinity, God in human form, the one who knows our suffering from the inside and em-bodies interpersonal love and intimacy. For them, God is male – partly because such a God meets their own perceived needs best and partly because this God is so closely identified with the person of Jesus of Nazareth.

It is not surprising that such different encounters with the immanent God lead to such different emphases on the purpose and character of the Church. The immanent God known in horizontal relationships with other beings, calls for the Church to enable and value horizontal relationships of community and communal action. The immanent God known in a personal encounter that retains a perceptible transcendent character, calls for the Church to be a space for the vertical relationship between the indi-vidual believer and her or his God. These differences are rein-forced by the different experiences of social life in middle-class areas as opposed to those on the working-class estates of East Newcastle. There is still a living sense of community within St Anthony's estate that provides the women I interviewed with a sense of rootedness and belonging (they may also appreciate these values within their church congregation, but this is not their primary source). In the more rootless life that characterises most middle-class professional Christians, there is a greater need to find community within the Church as it is not so readily apparent outside.

In both manifestations of the immanence of divinity, it is possible to find the impetus towards ethical action, although the direction may differ somewhat. Ecological issues connect most directly to an immanent divine who is present within the whole of the natural world, reinforcing the innate value of all living beings and the need for the flourishing of all to be considered. When the immanent divine is experienced in personal encounter, then it is the needs and flourishing of other human beings that are brought to the forefront of the mind. It is only when God is entirely transcendent, uninvolved with the life of the world, that ethical action is in real danger of being forgotten in favour of worshipful resignation. There is a need for balance within the practice of the Church so that there can be room for the relationship with God, especially for those whose lives are cluttered with family duties and access to places of spaciousness is limited, as well as relationships with one another, especially for those whose lives are fragmented and isolated.

Letty Russell's picture of the Church as round table and kitchen table does help to focus on the importance of fellowship and action. However, in order for such a Church to meet the needs of the women in my study, it would also need to include an altar table.[1] Feminist theology as a whole may be thought to have swung the pendulum too far in the direction of immanence and now needs to look at how transcendence can be usefully reincluded. This would give value to the experience of women for whom encounter with God involves transcendence along with immanence. It would also, as will become clear in the next section, allow a valuing of their understanding of the process and meaning of death.

It was apparent in the previous chapter that there was a wide gulf between the attitude to death characteristic of much feminist thought and that of the women in this study. While many feminist philosophers of religion and theologians wish to advocate the acceptance of finitude, seeing this as a positive move towards ethical action, the women in the interviews spoke of their reliance on a belief in a paradisial afterlife. In both cases, the concept of hope was central to their beliefs, but their hopes are very differently directed. The feminist hope is for a world where all people – and, indeed, all life forms – are able to flourish – a utopia that will only be brought about if people believe that this life is all there is and put all their energy into perfecting it. The hope of the women in the interviews is that this limited and painful world is *not* all there is, as they see no possibility of it allowing them to flourish to their full potential or that its perfecting could outweigh the pain of eternal separation from their loved ones.

Hope is often the most overlooked of the three theological virtues (the other two being faith and love), but it is an essential component of human flourishing. This can perhaps be seen most clearly by picturing life when hope is absent. This would either be a portrayal of flat despair or bleak resignation. In either case, it would not be a life that was motivated towards achieving our own flourishing or that of others, but one that focused solely on the needs of the day and short-term survival. There would be no expectation that the future could bring with it any good or that things could be improved by our own efforts. It may be that a hope wrongly focused is a better tool for human flourishing than no hope at all. This is not yet to say that either the feminist theologians or the local women have untenable systems of hope, but just to valorise the concept of hope as beneficial in its own right.

The question remains as to whether or not it is theologically justifiable for the local women to direct their hope to a world beyond this one rather than work for change within the only reality that we know for certain exists. Feminists might point to the deleterious results of such a belief in the past – seeing it, like Marx, as an opiate of the people that hinders all enthusiasm for social change. This allows Jantzen to outlaw such hope on the basis of her criteria of efficacy (theological truth is only valid where it contributes to human flourishing). However, this does not seem to be a full and fair assessment of the role that such hope plays in the lives of the women interviewed. Their hope enables them to cope with both the mourning process and the frustrations of their own lives. It is a hope that gives purpose and meaning by allowing them to define themselves against an eternal standard of judgement rather than the criteria of the current age. Their lives have worth because they are not defined by finitude but allowed to continue in growth towards fulfilment after life on this world has come to an end. This fulfilment continues their embodied and relational reality, as heaven is characterised as a place for the restoration and continuation of relationships with differently, but recognisably, embodied others.

This may mean that energies are directed towards personal salvation rather than social change, though it should be noted that only the evangelical Anglican women felt that salvation would depend more on their own actions than the merciful kindness of God towards all people. This hope may mean that the women are more tolerant of poor social conditions than they would otherwise be. As with much of the faith of the working-class women in the survey, it is more concerned with survival and flourishing as far as possible within the world as it is, than it is with transformation or greater potential flourishing for all in a utopian future.

It remains to be considered if, whatever its utility, belief in a continuation of life after death has any place within contemporary Christian thought. While it can be seen to conflict with the interests of eco-feminism, it could alternatively be seen to reinforce the emphasis on relationality. This would be a relationality where there was no sense that individuals were basically interchangeable – in other words, where the loss of one life would not be seen as being compensated for by the birth of another. Instead, it would be a relationality rooted in the reality of face-to-face relationships, involving a passionate connection with the intimate other. These relationships should be understood as constitutive of the individuals involved in them, as feminist thought has long argued, and as sites of a love that incarnates the divine. Further validation of such relationality comes from the belief of the women interviewed that such relationships are not bounded by death, but resonate eternally. The afterlife, in this understanding, is not about the survival of the lonely soul, but of the continuation of the person in relationships of love, both human and divine.[2] 'Heaven' is a community where personhood survives *in order that* relationality can survive.

Transcendence of the self, therefore, does not focus on the individual possessing an eternal soul that is divisible from the mortal body, but on the person being rooted in relationships of love that are caught up and into the relationality that is at the heart of God. Eternal being comes as the gift of the divine eternal, whose desire is to live in relationship with humanity and for humanity to mirror this relationality in its own relationships. This seems to offer a form of transcendence – and of life after death, – that is more in tune with feminist priorities than the classical model. It will not satisfy those whose philosophical convictions are centred on finitude, but may allow a conversation to continue between the Christianity of the working-class women interviewed and that of Christian feminist theologians. It would also allow value to be put on the quality of hope experienced by the women in the survey, even where that hope focuses on a site of value outside the material universe.

In the penultimate section of this chapter, I intend to make a little more apparent where my own theology fits in with the data that this research has uncovered. I write, it must be remembered, as an Anglican priest, so I have a deep investment in the Christian faith and can only write of it as an insider. Within the subdivisions of Christianity, I write as a feminist who feels more at home in the Catholic and radical sections of the Church than the evangelical and ultra-orthodox ones. In so far as a feminist position is a minority one within Christianity as a whole, and the Church of England as part of that whole, I write as one who is on the margins of the Church rather than at its centre. Like many other women, I struggle to remain true to both Christian understandings of the nature of God and feminist insights into the nature of reality. What follows will explain how I hold these two together and how this coupling has been influenced by my research for this book.

My own theology is unashamedly based in experience, though experience as held within and interpreted by the Christian tradition. This includes the sorts of spiritual experiences quoted by most of the women interviewed – an occasional sense of the presence of God, who is with me in an immediate and intense way, bringing affirmation and unconditional love. This mystical and emotional encounter with God needs to both inform intellectual speculation about the nature of God and be subjected to analysis itself. I have learnt from Joan Scott to see this experience not as a possession of mine to which I have free access, but as constitutive of both my self and my understanding of that self. As such, it necessarily plays a part in my understanding of my self in relation to God and so my understanding of the nature of God more generally.

The lens through which I view this experience is formed by both Christianity and feminism. In other words, I interpret my experiences with reference to those of many other people, past and present, who have understood God as love, personal and incarnate within the world, while also perceiving that this believing community has failed to take sufficient note of the insights and experiences of its female members. My experience of God is not limited to rare moments of mystical encounter, but is also mediated by the believing community and the wider world outside it. God is met in meeting other people, in the experiences of communal worship and communal action for justice, the awareness of the 'livingness' of all creation and in the scriptural story of God's interaction with the world – a mixture of revelation, interpretation and gross misunderstanding.

I found that the accounts of encounters with God as reported by the interviewees were both moving and affirmed my own moments of divine encounter. However, the way that I understand the God I encounter differs both from the understanding of the women in the interviews and many of the feminist writers on religious philosophy and theology. In many cases, it is not that our understandings are incompatible, it is that they contain different emphases. An example of this is the way that I and Marie (who we first met in Chapter 3), view our relationships with God. In both cases, the relationships are personal ones, characterised by love and affirmation, but, in Marie's case, it is gendered – passionately heterosexual and romantic – while mine is known as friendship. Marie's relationship with God is built on difference, with God being all that she is not – male, powerful and in control – while my relationship with God is built on alikeness, with God being inconceivably more than I am, but with God's image reflected in my female self. This is not a relationship of equals, but then neither is it one of dominance – there is the ability to work together and a gradual development of my own nature in a Godwards direction, an ability to see myself in the divine which is as much female as it is male.

This difference in perception relates to the difference in emphasis on the Holy Spirit in my theology as compared to that of the majority of the women interviewed, including Marie. Their experience of God as immanent concentrates on the relationship with Jesus, which offers them comfort and consolation but not divinisation. Seeing this reinforced my understanding of the place of the Spirit in my own spiritual experience, where it acts to uncover and develop the image of God and draw me closer into the living dance of the Trinity. My theology, therefore, calls for the inclusion of transformation within the divine–human relationship, rather than majoring on the support of the individual within the status quo.

This personal God provides for me the 'divine horizon' that Grace Jantzen advocates in a different form. I have also come to believe that the male image of God provides a 'divine horizon' for women like Marie. It is harder to reach because of the 'otherness' intrinsic to it, but offers a relational image that can be accessed via their own relationality. It is still not, however, an image that I can wholeheartedly embrace – not so much on the grounds of gender but on those of dominance and infantilism. This is still a God who needs to be placated and wooed, who does not allow the human self to be a fellow worker, instead keeping her as a subject – still a slave rather than an heir who offers affirmation but not the possibility of ultimate maturity in the acceptance of adult responsibility. I can see the strength that this image of God gives, but I remain outside its discursive power. God is certainly accessible in male language and imagery as well as female, but male God language, no less than female, still needs to mirror a God who calls us to be friends rather than servants.

Inherent to my own theology is the belief that each human person bears the image of God and one cannot be understood without the other. This means that God is to be seen in both women and men and it is idolatrous to limit God to either gender. It also means that each person can teach us something about God from the particular way in which they inhabit the divine image. This lesson was repeated with each woman I spoke to as they showed something new about the nature of God. We bear this image of God in our relationality – our ability to recognise and love the other – and, closely connected to this, our potential for transcendence. This idea of self is not far from that of the women interviewed, who see their lives in terms of relationships and eternity. However, the transcendence that I have in mind is rather different from theirs, as it is focused as much on this world as on the possibility of one to come.

In fact, my own view of transcendence builds on both the insights of the religious experiences of the women I met during the research and those of the feminist writers. Like Grace Jantzen, transcendence for me has a this-worldly aspect of a fulfilled embodiment and I would partly agree with her statement that, 'To have the capacity for transcendence does not entail having the capacity, now or in the future, to become disembodied, but rather to be embodied in loving, thoughtful, and creative ways.'[3] Such embodiment is valid and valuable in itself, but I would disagree with Jantzen's materialist conclusion that such relationality must end with the disintegration of the body. This is the natural conclusion if God is entirely immanent and this world is the only reality, but it does not follow if God is seen as retaining a transcendent dimension. In this context, the work of American theologian Marjorie Helen Suchocki offers a useful clarity with her insight that immanence means God co-experiences the world with us but is not irreducible to the world.[4]

I found this 'homeliness' of God, God experiencing alongside us, still apparent beneath the sense of God's transcendence in the women's recitations of their spiritual understanding. Although the focus of their hope is clearly the world to come, there is also a sense that they are companioned in this world by a loving divine presence. There are echoes here of the theology of Julian of Norwich: 'And this is the endless joy for us that our Lord means, that he will be our bliss when we are there, yet he is our keeper when we are here.'[5] This resonance with Julian provided another link with my own theology, influenced as it has been by her writings.

With Julian, and the women in this book, I would want to argue that we, by being caught up in the divine relational life that is God, are not irreducible to the world – that finitude is not the final word on humanity. This is not, I believe, because our bodies are the vehicles for an immortal soul, as classical dualism would suggest, but because the divine will is for relationality to continue and infinite worth to be placed on personhood. Like the majority of the women I talked to, I do not see a place for an infinity of punishment after death, although, again like them, I find it possible to believe in a time/place of continuing growth in love before full acceptance into the divine presence. It may also be that some individuals do not choose relationality and are allowed to opt for finitude instead. There remains a need for a healthy agnosticism about the possible details of continuing life, even while asserting it as a theological possibility. It is not, after all, supposed to be our major preoccupation or distract us from working for the flourishing of all that is here and now.

My perception of the location of God in relation to the world is more closely aligned to that of the moderate feminist theologians than the local women. Sallie McFague's panentheist God comes closest to my own understanding of how the world and God relate to one another. Like McFague, I find it important to keep the personal aspect of God, which allows conversation to continue both with the received Christian tradition and with women like those in the study for whom God is intensely personal. However, like McFague and unlike the women interviewed, I believe that we should primarily look for God in this world rather than beyond. As well as being approachable as the loving other, God is also the ground of being, the one who breathes through all living beings. In Ruether's language, God is both God and Gaia.

The women of St Anthony's see God as separate from the world, but also able to act decisively within it to alter the natural course and consequence of events. In this way, the world is, in fact, more under the control of God than in panentheist feminist theological thought, including my own. Eco-theology has rightly insisted on reminding us that the world is our responsibility and, as co-workers with God, we have been given the adult role of determining our own fate and that of the world, which has been entrusted to us. This world is a site where we encounter God, often in encounters with one another, but it is not a site that we can surrender to God's direct control. The question Anna asked me about why God does not answer her prayer to correct the relationship between her feuding sons[6] stayed with me and forced me to clarify my own thinking along the lines described above.

The research that leads to these conclusions uses a feminist methodology more rigorous than that employed by many writers of feminist theology and spirituality. By actually taking seriously the feminist injunction to listen to the voices of outsiders, especially female outsiders, it has raised questions about some of the conclusions feminist theologians have drawn regarding the beneficial and stifling aspects of the relationships between women and the divine. This concluding section goes on to outline some of the continuing questions and dilemmas that face the Church as it attempts to hold together the insights of academic theology and the spiritual experiences of the women and men in the pews. Any theological conclusions, therefore, should be seen as part of an ongoing process rather than as definitive answers to life's great questions.

It has been apparent from the outset of this book that there is a wide gap between the theological perceptions and spiritual understandings of the working-class women of the estates of New-castle and the writers of much contemporary academic theology – among whom we have focused on the feminist strand. It will have become apparent from the previous section that my own theology lies somewhere between the two, approaching one or the other more closely on different issues. It must be said that the emphasis on transcendence that was apparent during my research has had a large influence on my own thinking and reinforced my reluctance to embrace a theology where immanence completely displaces transcendence. The spirituality of immanence relies on an optimistic reading of the human situation, insisting on the possibility for transformation and fulfilment in this life, by human effort alone, and leaves unanswered the needs of those for whom such flourishing is not a possibility.

This book suggests that there is room – and a pressing need – for an openness in theology that prevents it becoming the domain of academics alone. Christian theology – especially where it is closely linked with spirituality – must take account of the experience of the divine of the whole Body of Christ, not just that segment of it to be found within the middle classes or even that small part within the academic or feminist fold. This means working with images of God that some may feel belong to the past, but still, nevertheless, provide support and self-esteem to women today. Into this category fall the images of God as exclusively masculine – both protective father and perfect lover – that appeared in the local women's testimonies and the language that they used for God. It is possible to see the value that such imagery has for women in these particular social circumstances and assert that, being beyond gender, God can be spoken of in male as well as female terms.

This male God is not a distant figure, despite the fact that he is believed to inhabit a heavenly realm. He is encountered in this world, able to be joked with and shouted at, and interested in the daily minutiae of the women's lives. Also, the heavenly realm cannot be said to be a totally alien place in these women's spiritualities. It is inhabited by their beloved dead, who may make the short journey back to our world to offer comfort and the reassurance of continued relationship. The human person is understood within an eternal dimension and given great value because of this – a value that is not shared by the rest of the created order. God's presence can also be an excuse for leaving the resolution of problems in his hands as he is believed to intervene directly in the world's affairs as his love will lead him to do.

The spirituality discovered in the interviews is one focused on survival – in this world, which has proved a harsh and difficult place to inhabit, and beyond death to enter a world where fulfilment and flourishing can finally take place. Feminist and ecological spirituality, on the other hand, focus on the potential and ethical needs of this world as the site for all human flourishing. Each spirituality emphasises relationships, although with very different meanings. Feminist and ecological thought see relationality as a web that encompasses all forms of life with which we share the planet and, as such, an unqualified good. The women who took part in the research see relationality as the ties that bind them to family and community, which are both positive and negative in their effects. God, in this context, is another being with whom they have a relationship. God, in ecological and feminist writings, is more often the force of relationality itself. Relationships for the local women are embodied in particular, proximate people rather than in any body and, being essentially relationships of eternal spirits one to another, do not extend to the animal world.

A spirituality of transcendent personhood has come up against a theology of immanent divinity in this book. In one strand, community is the starting point – taken for granted as a part of everyday life – while, for the other, community is a spiritual goal, to be nurtured in a theology of relationality and a pan(en)theistic divinity. Each is a spirituality and theology of love, but while one is characterised by romance, the other is marked by inclusivity. This is, of course, to deal in generalisations, which can distort almost as much as they reveal, but to do so gives something of the different flavour of the two sources of Christian thought on which this research is based.

The questions that remain are centred on how the Church and the academy are going to take forwards the theological project championed by feminist, liberation and ecological theologians. In order to be true to their own convictions, the first two at least have to make room for the voices of women and men with different agendas and priorities to their own. Further, it is entirely unrealistic – as womanist and lesbian feminist theologians have already made clear – to expect that such differing agendas and priorities will lead to similarly interpreted spiritual experiences. This then leaves the problem of how to include such disparate – even disapproving – voices within their own theological project.

There are two easy, but unacceptable, ways in which to resolve the dilemma. The first is to ignore, or devalue, the opinions of women and men who are not included within the feminist or liberation fold, refusing to allow their voices to be heard. This provides the conditions for the academy to continue to do theology *for* the women and men in the pews, who have not been privileged with our insights into their oppression and future liberation. If we take this path, then we are just imitating the very brands of theology that first excited feminist and liberationist mistrust. The second path is to relativise all theology so that it only applies to the group in which it has been produced. This leaves us with no possibility of making truth claims that apply beyond a very particular community and so inhibits liberation and feminist theology from speaking with an authoritative voice and undermines the possibility of working for positive change.

This debate is at the heart of feminist theory – theological and otherwise – at the present moment and is important for the wider theological arena as well. My research is part of this ongoing dialogue and echoes this key debate – the sense of being caught between the devil of exclusivity and the deep blue sea of complete relativity. It is not surprising, therefore, that, while I feel sure that to accept either of the above solutions would be to sell experience-based theology short, I am far less certain where the solution lies. Were we to lose either our willingness to listen to women and men outside the theological academy or our commitment to consider what we as feminist and liberation theologians believe best facilitates the flourishing of men and women, we would have brought the project of feminist and liberation theology to an inglorious end.

It is essential, therefore, that neither the listening nor the theological thinking stop. Those of us in the academy need to know where the men and women who form our congregations find strength in their faith and ensure that our theologising does not deprive them of a support that, in our particular situation, we may feel able to do without. We may even learn something about our own spiritual needs in the process. At the same time, we must respect our own standpoint and continue to develop the insights of our own position – not losing the vision of utopian change that has continually inspired feminist and liberationist writing. This listening and this thinking does not take place in isolation, but as part of a continuing dialogue with our scriptural and historical heritage. Experience-based theology that is radical, Christian and inclusive can only arise from all these processes being brought together in, hopefully creative, tension.

There is no easy compromise here, simply a realisation that the commitment to dialogue must continue. It is to be hoped that from such difficult conversations will arise the energy for continuing research that opens up the field of academic theology to new voices, and the Church as a whole to new theological insights. It is crucial that we take the risk of living with tension rather than prematurely resolving it so that new and fruitful thinking is not stifled before it is born.

The vision here is of a 'choral theology' – the Church singing not with one voice, but many. Unity comes from the fact that the Church is singing of the revelation of God via Jesus Christ and the Holy Spirit; it is this that provides the lyrics for our singing. However, the voices are not one but many, each singing the lyrics to the music that their experience of God has written into their Christian faith. This does not always add up to a completely harmonious sound – it is often far easier to hear the discord than recognise the basic unity of the song. The ultimate purpose of theology may be to provide the one tune that all can sing – one tune that is a true distillation of all the varied ways in which the people of God image God in their lives. Until that utopian moment, the necessity is to tune our ears to the vitality and variety of the present songs, as well as the music that has come down to us from the experiences of Christians who have gone before. Accepting the inevitable jumble of noise is a better way forward than to insist on a uniformity that silences certain voices altogether. The hope is that, by listening more carefully to the music that others are singing, we can tune all our voices to create greater harmony and draw nearer to that divine tune that resonates throughout the universe.

Notes

1 This might not be the best way in which to describe a worship space for the Methodist and evangelical women; perhaps a reading table, where the Bible would be placed, would have more resonance for them.
2 This reading necessarily fails to include the theology of the most evangelical of the women in the survey, who believed that salvation only involved the individual and God and that any other relationships would fail to signify after death.
3 *Becoming Divine: Towards a Feminist Philosophy of Religion*, Manchester: Manchester University Press, 1998, p. 271.

4 As stated in her essay 'God, sexism and transformation' in Rebecca S. Chopp and Mark Lewis Taylor (eds), *Reconstructing Christian Theology*, Minneapolis: Fortress, 1994, pp. 25–48.

5 From Chapter 77 of Julian of Norwich, *A Revelation of Love*, John Skinner (translator), Evesham: Arthur James, 1996, p. 152.

6 See Chapter 4.

POSTSCRIPT

The danger inherent in any use of metaphor or analogy is that it can be stretched further than it can feasibly go. I am very conscious of this possibility with my own use of 'choral' to describe a possible way forward for the theology of the Church. It is an image that is intended to provoke thought and discussion rather than to be seen as complete in itself. However, there may be a need to take the metaphor just a little further; in particular to consider who might fulfil the role of the conductor of such a diverse choir.

The conductor, in this instance, is to be seen as the one who ensures that all the members of a choir listen to each other. It is too ambitious to hope to be able to identify a conductor who could, at this stage of our theological and Church life, actually create a complete harmony out of the disparate voices. So, to step aside from the metaphor and back into actuality, how do we allow theologians and working-class women and men in the pews to encounter one another and to hear one another's contributions to our understanding of God? Or are we content to allow each section of the Church to go its own way without any reference to the others – to return to the metaphor, to allow the choir to sing their different lyrics in separate rooms?

My first instinct is to say that it is the clergy of all denominations who naturally inhabit a position between the academy and the pews, and that they might act as such conductors in their own areas. They live amongst the people they serve, sharing the same environment for the time that they are with them. They hope to be able to enter into their hopes and anxieties and learn the best language in which to speak to them about the reality of God. But their perspective remains distinct, even if they serve in a place which reflects their own social background and upbringing. They bring with them some degree of immersion in the waters of theological enquiry and an awareness of some at least of the currents within contemporary theological thought. Or that, at any rate, is the hope of theological educators across the denominations.

This is not only my vision for the clergy but that of the Archbishop of Canterbury, Rowan Williams, as he made clear in a talk given at the 150th anniversary of the founding of Ripon College, Cuddesdon (the oldest Anglican Theological College):

> And this leads into the second kind of responsibility, that of being an interpreter – by which I mean not primarily someone who interprets culture to and for the Church or interprets the Church's teaching to the world outside, but someone who has the gift of helping people make sense to and of each other. Communities, in spite of the sentimental way we sometimes think of them, don't just happen. They need nurture, they need to be *woven* into unity ... If the unity of the Church is not that of a mass of individuals with a few convictions in common but that of a differentiated organism where the distinctiveness of each is always already in play, then for the Church to be consciously itself, it needs people to see and show how diversity works together ... Put more theologically, it is about helping believers to see Christ in one another. The interpretative work of the priest looks first at how to uncover for one person or group the hidden gift in another – especially when the first impression is one of alienness and threat.[1]

This is exactly the job needed to be done by the conductor of a choral theology – the uncovering of the way that different groups and different individuals inhabit and make present the image of God. It is undeniable that there are clergy who are undertaking this work – I've met, and learnt from, a number of them. However, the trouble is that there are still many clergy who feel they are in place purely to instruct rather than to learn as well. They come to their post with the intention of teaching the congregation to sing according to their own theological lyric, rather than with the hope of hearing a fresh, indigenous psalm of praise to God which may blend with their own song to create something new. So, while they may bring some theology *to* their congregations, they are less likely to bring out the theological insights *from* their congregations. Their idea of the image of God is already set in concrete and is defended rather than re-examined when it comes into conflict with other images. Couple this with the depressingly familiar phenomenon of clergy who cease to read theology as soon as their training is behind them and it seems as if we may, sometimes if not always, need to look elsewhere for our conductors.

Such clergy as these are not the weavers of communities that Williams refers to later in his talk, but it may be that there are others within the Church who are already hoping to fill this role. Indeed, now we need to return to the very beginning of this book and to look again at the role that feminist theologians hope to play within the life of the Church and of the academy. Their two distinctive commitments are to listen to the voices of women and ensure that these are included within the thinking (and embodying and living out) of theology, and to strive for a world where theological commitment to issues of justice, peace and equality is reflected in real social change. Neither of these goals can be obtained by staying solely within the precincts of university life. This is especially true if we want to include voices of people from communities like St Anthony's estate. The older women, and many also of the younger generation, are deeply rooted in their locality and have neither the desire, nor the confidence and necessary academic achievements, to step far outside it. It is up to the more naturally peripatetic theologians to do the necessary crossing of boundaries – a process that is always easier when you are starting from a position of relative privilege rather than of relative powerlessness.

Perhaps one of the possible future paths for feminist theology is to see itself as a true theology for the Church rather than as a theology for other theologians. This would combine the two roles – of listening to others and acting for the kingdom of God – that are at the heart of Christian feminist writing; but in order for this to be achieved there are still considerable barriers to be overcome, and further questions to be asked. One of the hardest of these questions is that of how we encourage people to move away from what they are comfortable with and to encounter the image of God in seemingly alien form. I certainly find it easier to introduce the ideas of the women of St Anthony's to the wider theological world than I do to introduce the ideas of feminist theologians to the women of St Anthony's estate. Yet the traffic in theological thinking needs to go both ways if it is to be truly profitable – all parts of a choir need to listen to one another if they are eventually to sing together.

So this leads us on to one final answer to the question of who is to conduct this choir, and that is – *we* are. It may militate against the model to talk about multiple conductors but it does get closer to the reality of the situation in the Church today. We, as individual Christians, need to make the effort to listen to one another, both through reading and through talking together. We need to get to know how other Christians encounter God, and how their encounter can help us to understand our own. We need to become more expert at, in Rowan Williams' words, seeing 'Christ in one another', or, in my own words, recognising the image of God in the face of the other. This is work that we can all choose to undertake today, and it is work that is much needed within today's Church. Perhaps there will finally prove to be no need for the choir to be conducted if it can begin to listen to what God is saying in the other as well as to what God is saying in the Bible, in the tradition and in my own most secret heart.

Notes

1 Talk entitled 'The Christian Priest Today' and delivered at Ripon College, Cuddesdon, on 28 May 2004.

SELECT BIBLIOGRAPHY

Beattie, T., *God's Mother, Eve's Advocate: A Gynocentric Refiguration of Marian Symbolism in Engagement with Luce Irigaray*, Bristol: University of Bristol, 1999.

Bednarowski, M. F., *The Religious Imagination of American Women*, Bloomington: Indiana University Press, 1999.

Benhabib, S., J. Butler, D. Cornell and N. Fraser, *Feminist Contentions: A Philosophical Exchange*, New York: Routledge, 1995.

Brasher, B., *Godly Women: Fundamentalism and Female Power*, New Brunswick: Rutgers University Press, 1998.

Brown, C. G., *The Death of Christian Britain: Understanding Secularisation 1800–2000*, London and New York: Routledge, 2001.

Bruce, S., *Religion in Modern Britain*, Oxford: Oxford University Press, 1995.

Burdick, J., *Looking for God in Brazil: The Progressive Catholic Church in Urban Brazil's Religious Arena*, Berkeley: University of California Press, 1993.

Butler, J. and J. W. Scott (eds), *Feminists Theorize the Political*, London and New York: Routledge, 1992.

Cannon, K. G., A. M. Isasi-Díaz, K. Pui-Lan., L. M Russell (eds), *Inheriting Our Mothers' Gardens: Feminist Theology in Third World Perspective*, Louisville: Westminster, 1988.

Carr, A. E., *Transforming Grace: Christian Tradition and Women's Experience*, San Francisco: Harper & Row, 1988.

Chaturvedi, V., *Mapping Subaltern Studies and the Postcolonial*, London: Verso, 2000.

Chodorow, N., 'Family structure and feminine personality' in D. M. Juschka (ed.), *Feminism in the Study of Religion: A Reader*, London: Continuum, 2001, pp. 81–105.

Chopp, R. S. and M. L. Taylor (eds), *Reconstructing Christian Theology*, Minneapolis: Fortress, 1994.

Chopp, R. S. and S. G. Davaney (eds), *Horizons in Feminist Theology: Identity, Traditions and Norms*, Minneapolis: Fortress, 1997.

Clack, B., 'Revisioning death: a thealogical approach to the "evils" of mortality', *Feminist Theology*, **22**, September 1999, pp. 67–77.

Coakley, S. (ed.), *Religion and the Body*, Cambridge: Cambridge University Press, 1997.

Daly, M., *Beyond God the Father*, Boston: Beacon, 1973.

— *Gyn/Ecology: The Metaethics of Radical Feminism*, Boston: Beacon, 1978.

— *Pure Lust: Elemental Feminist Philosophy*, Boston: Beacon, 1984.

Fiorenza, E. S., *In Memory of Her: A Feminist Theological Reconstruction of Christian Origins*, London: SCM, 1983.

— 'The will to choose or to reject' in L. M. Russell (ed.), *Feminist Interpretation of the Bible*, Philadelphia: Westminster, 1995, pp. 125–36.

Fulkerson, M. M., *Changing the Subject: Women's Discourses and Feminist Theology*, Minneapolis: Fortress, 1994.

— 'Contesting the gendered subject: a feminist account of the *imago Dei*' in R. S. Chopp and S. G. Davaney (eds), *Horizons in Feminist Theology: Identity, Traditions and Norms*, Minneapolis: Fortress, 1997, pp. 99–115.

Gebara, I. and M. C. Bingemer, *Mary: Mother of God, Mother of the Poor*, P. Berryman (translator), Tunbridge Wells: Burns & Oates, 1989.

Gilligan, C., *In a Different Voice: Psychological Theory and Women's Development*, Cambridge, Massachusetts: Harvard University Press, 1982.

Graham, E., *Making the Difference: Gender, Personhood and Theology*, London: Mowbray, 1995.

Graham, E., and M. Halsey (eds), *Life Cycles: Women and Pastoral Care*, London: SPCK, 1993.

Grant, J., *White Women's Christ and Black Women's Jesus: Feminist Christology and Womanist Response*, Atlanta: Scholars, 1989.

Grey, M. C., *Redeeming the Dream: Feminism, Redemption, and Christian Tradition*, London: SPCK, 1989.

— *The Wisdom of Fools? Seeking Revelation for Today*, London: SPCK, 1993.

— *Prophecy and Mysticism: The Heart of the Postmodern Church*, Edinburgh: T. & T. Clark, 1997.

Griffith, R. M., *God's Daughters: Evangelical Women and the Power of Submission*, Berkeley: University of California Press, 1997.

Harding, S. and M. B. Hintikka (eds), *Discovering Reality: Feminist*

Perspectives on Epistemology, Metaphysics, Methodology, and Philosophy of Science, Dordrecht: D. Reidel, 1983.

Harris, H. A., 'Struggling for truth', *Feminist Theology*, **28**, September 2001, pp. 40–56.

Hogan, L., *From Women's Experience to Feminist Theology*, Sheffield: Sheffield Academic Press, 1995 (1964).

hooks, b, *'Ain't I A Woman?': Black Women and Feminism*, Boston: South End, 1981.

Irigaray, L., *The Sex Which Is Not One*, C. Potter (translator), New York: Cornell University Press, 1977.

—— 'Equal to whom?', R. L. Mazzola (translator) in K. Ward (ed.), *The Postmodern God: A Theological Reader*, Oxford: Blackwell, 1997, pp. 198–213.

Jantzen, G. M., *Power, Gender and Christian Mysticism*, Cambridge: Cambridge University Press, 1995.

—— *Becoming Divine: Towards a Feminist Philosophy of Religion*, Manchester: Manchester University Press, 1998.

Jenkins, T., *Religion in English Everyday Life: An Ethnographic Approach*, New York: Berghahn, 1999.

Johnson, E. A., *She Who Is: The Mystery of God in Feminist Theological Discourse*, New York: Crossroad, 1992.

—— *Friends of God and Prophets: A Feminist Theological Reading of the Communion of Saints*, London: SCM, 1998.

Jones, S., *Feminist Theory and Christian Theology: Cartographies of Grace*, Minneapolis: Fortress, 2000.

—— 'Hope deferred: theological reflections on reproductive loss (infertility, miscarriage, stillbirth)', *Modern Theology*, **17**:2, April 2001, pp. 227–45.

Julian of Norwich, J. Skinner (translator), *A Revelation of Love*, Evesham: Arthur James, 1996.

Kerber, L. et al., 'On *In a Different Voice*: an interdisciplinary forum' in D. M. Juschka (ed.), *Feminism in the Study of Religion: A Reader*, London: Continuum, 2001, pp. 106–33.

Kitzinger, C., and S. Wilkinson, 'Theorizing representing the other' in S. Wilkinson and C. Kitzinger (eds), *Representing the Other: A Feminism and Psychology Reader*, London: Sage, 1996, pp. 1–32.

Kyung, C. H., *Struggle to be the Sun Again: Introducing Asian Women's Theology*, New York: Orbis, 1990.

Langford, W., *Revolutions of the Heart: Gender, Power and the Delusions of Love*, London: Routledge, 1999.

McFague, S., *Metaphorical Theology: Models of God in Religious Language*, London: SCM, 1983.

— *Life Abundant: Rethinking Theology and Economy for a Planet in Peril*, Minneapolis: Fortress, 2001.

McRae, S., (ed.), *Changing Britain: Families and Households in the 1990s*, Oxford: Oxford University Press, 1999.

Mechthild of Magdeburg, F. Tobin (translator), *The Flowing Light of the Godhead*, New York: Paulist, 1998.

Nicholson, L. (ed.), *Feminism/Postmodernism*, New York: Routledge, 1990.

Northcott, M. (ed.), *Urban Theology: A Reader*, London: Cassell, 1998.

Pearce, L. and J. Stacey (eds), *Romance Revisited*, London: Lawrence & Wishart, 1995.

Plaskow, J. and C. P. Christ (eds), *Womanspirit Rising: A Feminist Reader in Religion*, San Francisco: HarperCollins, 1979.

— (eds), *Weaving the Visions: New Patterns in Feminist Spirituality*, San Francisco: Harper & Row, 1989.

Pui-Lan, K., *Introducing Asian Feminist Theology*, Sheffield: Sheffield Academic Press, 2000.

Radway, J., *Reading the Romance: Women, Patriarchy and Popular Literature*, Chapel Hill: University of North Carolina Press, 1984.

Rich, A., *Of Woman Born: Motherhood as Institution and Experience*, London: Virago, 1976.

Roberts, E., *Women and Families: An Oral History, 1940–1970*, Oxford: Blackwell, 1995.

Rosser, C., and C. C. Harris, *The Family and Social Change: A Study of Family and Kinship in a South Wales Town*, London: Routledge & Kegan Paul, 1983.

Ruether, R. R., *New Woman, New Earth: Sexist Ideologies and Human Liberation*, 2nd edition, Boston: Beacon, 1995.

— *Sexism and God-Talk*, Boston: Beacon, 1983.

— *Women and Redemption: A Theological History*, London: SCM, 1998.

— *Christianity and the Making of the Modern Family*, Boston: Beacon, 2000.

Sawyer, D. F. and D. M. Collier (eds), *Is There a Future for Feminist Theology?*, Studies in Theology and Sexuality 4, Sheffield: Sheffield Academic Press, 1999.

Schneider, S., 'Spirituality as an academic discipline: reflections from experience' in M. A. Tilley and S. A. Ross (eds), *Broken and Whole: Essays on Religion and the Body*, New York: University Press of America, 1993, pp. 207–18.

Schillebeeckx, E., *Mary, Mother of the Redemption*, London: Sheed & Ward, 1964.

Scott, J. W., 'Experience' in J. Butler and J. W. Scott (eds), *Feminists Theorize the Political*, New York: Routledge, 1992, pp. 22–40.

Shepherd, L. M., *Feminist Theologies for a Postmodern Church: Diversity, Community and Scripture*, New York: Peter Lang, 2002.

Shilling, C., *The Body and Social Theory*, London: Sage, 1993.

Sjørup, L., 'Mysticism and gender', *Journal of Feminist Studies in Religion*, Fall 1997, **13**:2, pp. 45–68.

— *Oneness: A Theology of Women's Religious Experiences*, Leuven: Peeters, 1998.

Skeggs, B., *Formations of Class and Gender*, London: Sage, 1997.

Stanley, L. and S. Wise, *Breaking Out: Feminist Consciousness and Feminist Research*, London: Routledge & Kegan Paul, 1983.

Strathern, M., *After Nature: English Kinship in the Twentieth Century*, Cambridge: Cambridge University Press, 1992.

Suchocki, M. H., 'God, sexism and transformation' in R. S. Chopp and M. L. Taylor (eds), *Reconstructing Christian Theology*, Minneapolis: Fortress, 1994, pp. 25–48.

Thistlethwaite, S. B., *Sex, Race and God: Christian Feminism in Black and White*, New York: Crossroad, 1989.

Thistlethwaite, S. B. and M. P. Engel (eds), *Lift Every Voice: Constructing Christian Theologies from the Underside*, 2nd edition, Maryknoll, New York: Orbis, 1998.

Turner, B. S., *Religion and Social Theory*, 2nd edition, London: Sage, 1991.

Ward, G. (ed.), *The Postmodern God: A Theological Reader*, Oxford: Blackwell, 1997.

Warner, M., *Alone of All Her Sex*, London: Picador, 1990.

Watson, N. K., *Introducing Feminist Ecclesiology*, London: Continuum, 2002.

Whitford, M. (ed.), *The Irigaray Reader*, Oxford: Blackwell, 1991.

Wilkinson, S. and C. Kitzinger (eds), *Representing the Other: A Feminism and Psychology Reader*, London: Sage, 1996.

— *Breaking Out Again: Feminist Ontology and Epistemology*, London: Routledge, 1993.

Williams, D. S., 'Womanist theology: black women's voices' in J. Plaskow and C. P. Christ (eds), *Weaving the Visions: New Patterns in Feminist Spirituality*, San Francisco: Harper & Row, 1989, pp. 179–86.

— *Sisters in the Wilderness: The Challenge of Womanist God-Talk*, New York: Orbis, 1996.

Woodhead, L., 'Spiritualizing the sacred: a critique of feminist theology', *Modern Theology*, **13**:2, 1997, pp. 191–212.

— 'Feminist theology – out of the ghetto?' in D. F. Sawyer and D. M. Collier (eds), *Is There a Future for Feminist Theology?*, Studies in Theology and Sexuality 4, Sheffield: Sheffield Academic Press, 1999, pp. 198–206.

Woodhead, L., and P. Heelas, *Religion in Modern Times: An Interpretative Anthology*, Oxford: Blackwell, 2000.

Young, M. and P. Wilmot, *Family and Kinship in East London*, London: Routledge & Kegan Paul, 1957.

Zappone, K., *The Hope for Wholeness: A Spirituality for Feminists*, Mystic, Connecticut: Twenty-Third Publications, 1991.

INDEX